THE CATHARS & REINCARNATION

ARTHUR GUIRDHAM

The Cathars &
Reincarnation

Al cap des set cens ans verdegeo le
laurel
After seven hundred years the laurel
will be green again

SAFFRON WALDEN
THE C. W. DANIEL COMPANY LTD

First published in Great Britain by
Neville Spearman Publishers

This edition published by
The C. W. Daniel Company Limited
1 Church Path, Saffron Walden, Essex. CB10 1JP, England
in 1990

© *Arthur Guirdham 1970*

ISBN 0 85207 224 4

Set in 11 on 13pt Juliana

Produced in Great Britain by
Ennisfield Print & Design, London

To My Wife

FOREWORD

It is impossible to mention all those to whom I am indebted in the production of this book. In writing it I had to assume the, for me, unusual rôle of a research student in history. I could not have acquired all the information I needed without help from others. I am chiefly indebted to Professor René Nelli, formerly professor of mediaeval studies at the University of Toulouse, and to Monsieur Jean Duvernoy. In letters and encounters over five years Professor Nelli has rendered me inestimable service in verifying the statements made by Mrs. Smith in her dreams and revelations. Contact with him also stimulated me to increase my knowledge of, and insight into, the aims and philosophy of Catharism.

I owe a tremendous debt to Monsieur Jean Duvernoy whose works, along with those of Professor Nelli, are enumerated in the bibliography. Monsieur Duvernoy has never failed to supply me with valuable information, particularly with regard to the close-knit relationship between the families involved in my story. In the late Summer of 1969 when I visited the Languedoc, Monsieur Duvernoy not only read this book to exclude the possibility of historical errors but also gave up the best part of three days to increasing my education.

Mademoiselle Josette Lamé and Ash Hanson were immensely and productively helpful in commenting on the mediaeval songs recorded by Mrs. Smith.

I am also grateful to Miss Madge Lovell, who typed this book, for her repeat performance of the perpetual miracle of reading my handwriting, to my wife for typing intricate insertions and footnotes, to Brenda Smith and Quentin Guirdham for their scrutiny of the finished product, to Mr. Ian Macdonald and the Reverend K. B. Flenley for translating the depositions in Latin, and to Peter Pagan and the staff of the Bath Libraries for their amazing persistence and conscientiousness in obtaining, from all manner of sources, the books I required for my researches.

I do not need to say that I am indebted to Mrs. Smith for the remarkable and copious raw material with which she supplied me.

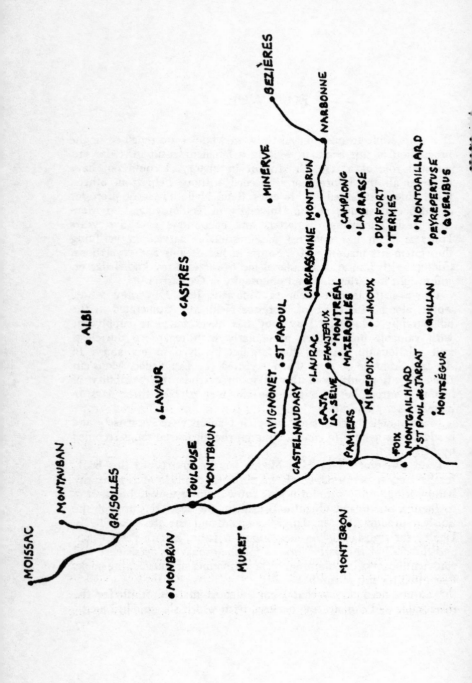

I

Though I try always to write from practical experience, in my previous books some reasoning and interpretation have been necessary. It is therefore a relief to write without calling into play these two faculties. All I intend is to tell a story. In so doing I am spared even exercising the imagination. The story I am writing is true.

This is not just another tale of reincarnation. The justification for writing it is that its origins and substance are unique. So many accounts of reincarnation are personal memories. One has to decide for oneself, from the subject matter and its mode of presentation, whether the experience is valid and the author a person of integrity. In another species of reincarnation story defects and symptoms in a present lifetime are connected neatly with experiences in a previous existence. If I chose I could build my story round this theme. But because reincarnation explains logically and justly why we suffer in a particular way in this life is no proof of its truth. Because a theory seems reasonable or because it answers a need should not make it acceptable.

One of the striking characteristics of this story is that I myself have no personal recollection of my incarnation which can nevertheless be accurately placed in the first half of the thirteenth century in the Languedoc. This was revealed through the dreams and visions of a patient. In order to regard her experiences as valid, one would expect her to have a knowledge of the mode of life in the Languedoc of the thirteenth century, and to have acquired this by direct experience, through visions, dreams and intuitions, without having studied the period or subject. The major proporton of her revelations occurred twenty-six years ago, in an intensive uprush of memory in her early teens. It gave her a detailed knowledge of Catharism, though until she met me she was even unaware of the name of this heresy. She also acquired a vivid realisation of life in the Languedoc in the thirteenth century. Neither mediaeval history nor literature were taught in her school. Twenty-five years ago the history and ritual of Catharism were not imparted to girls of thirteen in English grammar schools. The same applies today. At the present time little enough is known of Catharism in this country. Its ritual and practice are known to a few savants and sympathisers. The number of these was still smaller a quarter of a century ago. Nor is it, nor has it even been, a practice for English girls of thirteen to transcribe their thoughts, visions and feelings in mediaeval French or in the quite distinct language of the Langue d'Oc.

But I have still more important proof of the reality of the experience I intend to describe. Twenty-six years ago this girl knew and noted in writing what was unknown to any of those who had written on this subject in any language, in the seven centuries which have elapsed since the eclipse of this so-called heresy. All writers who mentioned the subject insisted that the robes of Cathar priests were inevitably black. For twenty-six years, including her six years correspondence with me, she stubbornly maintained that they wore dark blue. She was proved correct by Jean Duvernoy of Toulouse but only in the last four years. In editing the register of the Inquisition of Jacques Fournier, Monsieur Duvernoy revealed that Cathar priests wore sometimes dark blue or dark green. This book was published in 1965.[1] The truth was known to my patient as far back as 1944. She expressed it in writing more than a year before the publication of Duvernoy's book.

The really unique feature of this book is that I have only acted as an amateur historian in checking what my patient has revealed. In so doing I have discovered the details of my previous existence. When I wrote to Monsieur Jean Duvernoy, the chief authority in France, and probably in the world, on the history of Catharism, he expressed his astonishment at my detailed knowledge of the subject. I could not tell him I had obtained it from a schoolgirl's notes of her dreams and visions. Until five years ago I had no detailed knowledge of the subject, though for more than thirty years the names Cathar and Albigensian[2] have had a haunting quality for me.[3]

Is this story evidence of reincarnation? Is some other explanation, for instance, that of thought transference, applicable? The answer is no. The patient's major experiences were a quarter of a century ago at a time when I had no detailed knowledge of Catharism. In the last five years I had nothing to transfer to her. I did not know the characters she described. I heard of them first

[1] Le Registre d'Inquisition de Jacques Fournier. Introduction et notes par Jean Duvernoy. Privat Toulouse. 1965.

[2] For general purposes and for the non-specialist reader, Cathar and Albigensian can be regarded as alternative definitions. Cathar, meaning pure, is a description expressed in religious terms. The implications of the word Albigensian are geographical and designed to convey that the heresy was predominant in the country round Albi. This is not strictly accurate but the word Albigensian has nevertheless become part of the currency of history.

[3] At the end of September and the beginning of October, 1969, Monsieur Duvernoy read the manuscript of this book and discussed it with me on three occasions. He said the book contained no historical errors. He said that in one or two places there were alternative possibilities but only on minor issues. For instance, I describe Mir de Camplong as having estates in Camplong in the Corbières. Monsieur Duvernoy points out that another place called Camplong exists in the Languedoc but that the matter is not important because it was equally a centre of heresy.

11

from her. Then I discovered about them later in works of reference.

This story is no luxuriant recollection of myself as being a King of Babylon consorting with a beggar maid. (It is interesting how often stories of reincarnation involve the teller having been a romantic or elevated personage.) It is more interesting, more real and more tragic. It is really the patient who tells the story. I had to do more reading than I wished in order to verify it. At first sight what one set out to achieve seemed fantastic. I had to begin from the clue, 'If anything should happen to me you must go to Fabrissa'. To begin with I had to find out whether Fabrissa was the name of a person or a place and, if the former, whether she or he was related to an obscure character called Pierre de Mazerolles. A slight difficulty was that one had to search for information across the gulf of seven centuries. One established beyond doubt that Fabrissa was the name of a woman and that she was the aunt of the said Pierre de Mazerolles.

2

My first acquaintance with Catharism was in 1938. In that year I read a little about the Albigensians in Ford Madox Ford's *Provence*. This book was an insecure guide in that the author had no deep appreciation of the philosophy of Catharism. He regarded the Cathars as tolerant and civilised humanists with strong anti-Catholic convictions but did not stress the positive aspect of their religion. His book, as a guide to Catharism, was of no value to me but it acted as an enzyme which initiated a thirty years process of inner fermentation.

The book also aroused in me a burning desire to go to Provence. I did so and found the countryside strangely compelling. My reaction was interesting in that I had previously insisted on spending my holidays in high mountains. In Provence I visited only the plains or the low hills around Les Baux. Yet when the war came it was the region above all others which aroused in me the pain of separation. In the succeeding years there were all kinds of vague pointers but none of great import. Years before I met my patient, in some of the books I have written, references to the Cathars were dragged in with wild irrelevance. Nor do I know why, in wartime England, I bought a large and detailed guide book of Carcassonne, one of the great centres of the heresy. The book was in French. I did not know the language. The people responsible for my education were sufficiently misguided to teach me German. I began to teach myself French in 1943. Consideration of such matters is influenced by hindsight and should not be taken too seriously, but I think my wartime yearning for Provence and the fact that the Midi had replaced my passion for the Alps are facts of some significance.

Provence was, though not entirely a false start, an error in direction. Catharism was common in Provence but reached its maximum intensity in the Languedoc. Before the seven centuries —dead Cathars began to interfere with my life, I was haunted by the longing to see Montségur.[1] I use the word haunted deliberately because years before I knew anything of its history, I longed to see it but somehow I made no effort to do so. It is clear that I wished to defer my visit. There was an element of fear in my yearning, though at this time I did not know that the Cathars had been burnt there but only that it was in some way sacred. After I had seen the Pyrenees, including Montségur, for the first time, I knew that my preoccupation with Provence was minimal compared with the compulsion exercised on me by the Pyrenees and Languedoc.

My wife pointed out to me that before we went to the Pyrenees I had always a reluctance to return on holiday to the same place, even if we had greatly enjoyed it. My argument had always been that there were other beautiful places to see and that we could return to our previous ports of call when we were older. Since I first visited the south-west of France I have never

---

[1] The peak on the lower slopes of which two hundred Cathar Parfaits were burnt. A Parfait was a Cathar priest purified by having bestowed on him the exclusively Cathar sacrament known as the Consolamentum.

wanted to go elsewhere, though sometimes I have been held back from returning by a feeling, hard to define, easy to pass off as procrastination and cowardice, but perhaps not wholly unwise and which I can best describe as a vague intuition of not being quite ripe for something.

I never gave reincarnation a thought before 1962.

For what it is worth the Eastern Pyrenees, the low wild hills called the Corbières, and the country round Carcassonne, Fanjeaux and Montréal, have for me a burning intensity which endows the earth with life to a degree I have not experienced elsewhere. Montségur is different. It has a green, ethereal beauty with great peace, yet with a great power of magnetism and also the capacity to induce a heartache. This is not sentiment. It could well be aesthetic feeling. I may have discovered two types of landscape especially suited to my make-up. It could also be memory. But as I say I do not claim to remember. Nevertheless I went back without knowing or remembering to the town house of my thirteenth-century grandfather. With an equal lack of intention I came upon his castle in the country. I only discovered later that I had been drawn to places which centuries ago must have been very familiar to me.

3

The story begins in March, 1962. This was the first occasion on which I saw Mrs. Smith. It was obvious from the doctor's letter that he had not thought her a pressing case but had referred her to a psychiatrist because he had been asked to do so. The story was simple. She suffered from a nightmare accompanied by shrieks so loud that she and her husband feared that she would awake the street. The dream was not of any particular interest. A man entered her room from the right side. She was lying on the floor. His approach filled her with terror. Sometimes there were one or two other details attached to the dream but these

14

she only revealed later and its basic substance is as I have stated. She had had this dream for twenty years. When it first began it had occurred once every so many months but over the years it had intensified until, during the months preceding her visit, it had come two or three times weekly. The patient was in her early thirties. She was good-looking, open, communicative and smiling. She was an earnest and eager talker but did not give the appearance of any great tension.

In looking at the case notes enclosed by her doctor I was surprised to find that she had had in her early teens a few attacks of unconsciousness and that she had been referred to a neurologist. He had ordered an encephalogram. This had given one of the varieties of positive result and she had been diagnosed as an epileptic. I felt convinced that this woman was not epileptic. Of course I did not know at this time that her attacks of unconsciousness began at the same age as her dreams and revelations. I had no idea that she had any extra-sensory capacities. My refusal to accept her as epileptic was reasonable enough. Doctors can disagree as to a diagnosis. In addition, she had only three attacks in the course of a year, following which they disappeared completely. It was many years since she had seen the neurologist and there had been no recurrence. What was interesting and strange was that, in spite of the neurologist's opinion and my own cautious nature, I wrote a letter to her doctor saying not only that she was not epileptic but that on no account should the encephalogram be repeated. I was perfectly justified in expressing my opinion as to diagnosis. My instructions *not* to repeat the encephalogram are curious. I could have taken the view that, seeing that it was years since the patient had had an attack and that her total score was three, the whole matter was best disregarded. I could also have suggested a repeat encephalogram or, alternatively, I could have avoided in my letter to the doctor any allusion to the subject. I wrote as I have indicated because I was convinced, for no entirely rational reason, that epilepsy was out of the picture, in spite of the previous positive encephalogram, and that the latter should not be repeated.[1]

After this first interview the patient's dream disappeared never to return, though I did not learn this till eighteen months later. This disappearance, after one encounter, of nightmares which have lasted years, is a form of psychic communication. If I do not enlarge on this theme it is because I am limiting myself to telling a story.

Another curious fact arises in relation to Mrs. Smith's dream. For years of my life I suffered from a particularly horrifying nightmare. In it a tall man approached the place I was sleeping. He came from behind me on the left. Sometimes he bent over me. I felt rigid and speechless with panic. My wife tells me that often I screamed loudly in this nightmare. As far as I can estimate this affliction began in my twenties. In my middle years it occurred perhaps three or four times a year. It became more frequent in my late fifties. At the same time it became less terrifying. Sometimes in my dream I was able to sit up and confront my visitor. The last time it occurred I was able to tell him that now I was ready for him.

Though I cannot be certain as to when my nightmare started I can be infinitely more accurate about its cessation. This occurred a short time, perhaps up to a few months, before or after I met Mrs. Smith. My recurrent nightmare was similar though not identical with hers. It had bothered me for between thirty and forty years. It ceased within a few months, or it may have been weeks, of my meeting her. Is this significant? Not in itself but the reader may later draw his own conclusions against the background of the other facts revealed in this book. I feel that my nocturnal visitor was the same man who disturbed Mrs. Smith's dreams.

I saw the patient in May and August of 1962 and in February 1963. On each occasion she described herself as well. It was

[1] From this patient, and from others like her, I have learnt that seemingly epileptic reactions in adolescents can indicate the latter's capacity to step out of time. In such cases the apparent epileptic tendency disappears as the patient matures.

16

obvious she was better and much happier. On one occasion she revealed that her nightmares had ceased but she did not tell me that they had done so after her first visit. Her reasons for abstaining from doing so will appear in the course of this narrative.

4

I could not have written this book had I not started to keep a diary on the 25th October, 1963. As will be seen later this was well before I began to be chased by the Cathars or before I knew anything of Mrs. Smith's Cathar allegiances. This diary was by no means a social history. It was a record of my inner life and in it I noted cases of extra-sensory perception and any examples of mysticism and psychic communication which I encountered. I also recorded any of my dreams which I thought significant and which I remembered easily. I have never practised the systematic recording of dreams nor am I specially interested in their inter-pretation. Without this journal I could not have produced this book nor could I have gained the increased though minimal insight into myself which I achieved by writing it.

I only kept this diary in any kind of strict form for two years and even then I did not achieve anything like a daily entry. After that I began to let it slide. It had served its purpose, which was to demonstrate to me the realities of psychic communication and how, during the periods when this is operating, all manner of extra-sensory manifestations in others are related to an 'open' state in oneself. This latter condition is unwilled and one is unaware of it while it is operating. In 1966 and 1967 the entries are fewer and in 1968 they were indeed sparse and not very illuminating.

When I began this diary I had clearly in mind my reasons for so doing. This is not to say that I argued myself into the necessity for keeping a journal. The reasons for so doing came to me clearly and without effort. Firstly, I wished to know if there was a kind of psychic thread tying this and that event together over certain periods of time. From this I hoped to discover whether there were 'open' periods in which communication was active and others in which contact was broken. Thirdly, I felt that, at this time of my life, anybody with whom I became especially acquainted had a particular significance for me or was in some way bound to me or had something to teach me.

In July of the year following, 1964, I met Professor Nelli of Carcassonne who lectures at the University of Toulouse. He is the best known exponent of the metaphysics of Catharism and probably the greatest living interpreter of the poetry of the troubadours.[1] When on my second visit to Professor Nelli he wished to verify that he had my address in England, he added, 'But of course I have. I put it down in my diary.' He then told me he had started a diary and gave as his reasons for so doing those which had impelled me to begin my own. He expressed verbally the identical thoughts which had formed in my mind. He was also sure that there were certain months in which things happened to him more frequently than in others. His own special month was May. He anticipated me by five months and started his diary in May, 1963.

It is interesting that in November, 1963, a month after I had started my diary, I had a letter from Lawrence Durrell saying that in my book *The Nature of Healing* I had thrown away a wonderful theme and had wasted my opportunities by too hasty treatment. He advised that I would do far better writing in the form of a doctor's diary. (He threw in poetical allegory as a possible alternative but I felt this was beyond my capacity.) I did not inform him that I had accepted his suggestion before he had uttered it and that the first entry in my diary was October 25th.

[1] There is a close relationship between Catharism and the cult of the troubadours. Many of the noble families converted to Catharism were also patrons of the troubadours.

5

The story gains momentum on the 13th December, 1963. I throw this as a sop to those who may regard this journal as an example of human credulity. Many people regard Friday the thirteenth as unlucky but if lucky numbers existed, which emphatically they don't, certainly thirteen would be mine. When I was young I had a habit of being put at desks labelled thirteen in the course of examinations and on such occasions I invariably did well.

On this date I went after out-patients to have my regular weekly tea with Mrs. A. The entry in my diary for that day begins, 'Recently I have felt dry and not at all "open".' It continues to the effect that I had had a good deal of harassing work but that there had been a 'couple of intimations'. A few nights previously I had dreamt of Falmouth. The next morning I received a letter from a woman in that town telling me that some Tibetan monks were going to a place in Dorset. This lady had written once previously but was not a regular correspondent. I had been interested in Buddhism in a tentative way for nine or ten years previously. This never amounted to more than desultory and piecemeal reading of simple books on the subject, always dodging any theological complexities. My diary records that I thought the time was propitious to meet them in Dorset. The significance of Buddhism in my story will be apparent later.

As to the second intimation there is a note to the effect that I could not remember it! My diary was, even at its best, a desultory affair, depending not only on whether anything was happening but on whether I had time to record it. It would be wildly inaccurate to infer that I had a set theme and a charted course, and that the function of my diary was to put in the details.

On this particular day, in the course of tea, I began to speak of a place called Little Gaddesden in Hertfordshire. I do not know how I got on to the subject. Mrs. A, my hostess, had years ago lived in the vicinity. I used to go walking there not long after

I qualified. At that time I had no idea of Mrs. A's existence. I tried to remember the name of the inn where I used to have lunch. I could not do so, nor could Mrs. A. I became very preoccupied with the name of the inn and kept on asking her if she recollected it. I must have been a bit of a bore.

After I left I decided suddenly to go to the public library. I wanted a travel book about the Pyrenees. At out-patients that afternoon I had seen Mrs. Smith. It transpired in the course of conversation that she had visited that part of the world for a holiday. I asked her about the scenery and said that I was also interested in that region from the historical point of view. I mentioned that one of my historical interests was a heretical sect called the Cathars. I do not know why I should have made this statement. It was not remotely likely that an out-patient seen at long intervals should have any interest in the subject. At this time I had no knowledge whatever of Mrs. Smith's far memories or of any of her nightmares other than the simple one described previously. It should equally be understood that she herself had at that time no realisation whatever that she had been a Cathar. Her ignorance of mediaeval history was such that though she recollected perfectly and in detail certain Cathar rituals, she did not know that they characterised a particular sect to which she had belonged. More than this, she had not encountered the name Cathar till earlier that afternoon, in fact a little before she was brought in to see me. On previous occasions at out-patients she had been kept waiting beyond her time of appointment. She decided to go to the library and get a book to read while she waited. She picked up a book on French mediaeval history, opened it at random at a section dealing with the Cathars, found the whole subject absorbing and, as she told me later, nearly jumped out of her skin when I used the word to her. Her surprise must obviously have been more than that provoked by mere coincidence. She must at this stage of her life have become habituated to the idea that certain synchronisations of circumstances must have a special significance for her. She had realised in her early teens that she was different from other people. At this time I myself was unaware of her make-up.

My motive in raising the question of the Pyrenees was simply because I wanted to know if she thought the country beautiful. Behind my reference to the Cathars was, to some extent, the desire to pose the question. 'Have you been to Montségur?' but I was too diffident to do so. One does not habitually put questions, about things which have haunted one for years, to people seen infrequently at out-patients. In any case I did not have Mrs. Smith in mind when I went to the library.

There were two travel books about the Pyrenees. I looked at one and rejected it. It was only when I got home that I discovered that the second contained material about the Cathars. I sat down to read for a few minutes before my evening meal. Practically at once I came across a reference to Little Gaddesden and the name of the inn which had been tantalising me at teatime. I was quite astonished. I could not have anticipated finding details of a Hertfordshire village in a work devoted to the Pyrenees. I read eagerly. The author described how, on two successive nights, she had heard what she described as French of a kind coming up from outside her window. She found this experience disturbing and was relieved when a friend, commenting on her startled appearance and extracting a confession of its cause from her, admitted that she herself had had the same experience.

The village of Little Gaddesden is close to Ashridge Manor. The latter is on the site of a thirteenth-century monastery. The crypt, an old well and one or two pieces of old wall are all that remains of the thirteenth-century foundations.

My diary for that day contains on two successive lines the following disconnected sentences. 'I must follow up my ancestry one day' and 'I must also study a bit about the Bonshommes'.

The name Bonshommes was that given to the Cathar priests in the Languedoc and elsewhere by the people to whom they ministered. The monastery at Ashridge belonged to the Order of Bonshommes. So far, so good. And Todd's history of Ashridge mentions that the monastery was founded by monks of heretical persuasion from the South of France. It would be nice to think

21

that one had holed out in one, but in actual fact researches I made later proved that, so far as Ashridge is concerned, the case for it being a Cathar foundation must be regarded on the available evidence as non proven. There was a Catholic Augustinian Order of Bonshommes with houses in Ashridge, Edlington and Bristol.[1] This Order was founded in the early thirteenth century. The date for Ashridge itself is 1270. It is hardly likely that a Cathar foundation could have been established openly in England at such a time, when Catharism in France had been practically exterminated earlier in the century, though it persisted up till the early fourteenth century in such places as Albi and the Upper Ariège. Furthermore Cathars had already been tried and persecuted in England at Oxford in 1160.[2]

The Black Prince owned a castle near Berkhampsted which is in the immediate vicinity of Ashridge. It has been suggested[3] that the Royal House at that time were not only tinged with heresy —the Black Prince himself could have been contaminated during his campaigns in Aquitaine—but also that they were antagonistic to the de Montfort family, which included the hammer of the Cathars. For this reason it had been surmised that the Plantagenets may have been sympathetic to a Cathar foundation. I would, however, need a good deal more evidence before I, personally, could accept such a view. As my rôle in this story is to act as an amateur of historical research, and as the amateur is usually more Roman than the Romans, one has at this juncture to reject the idea of a Cathar foundation at Ashridge. Yet I persist and forecast that one day it will be proved that there was Cathar influence at this place.

On this date, December 13th, my diary contains the remark, 'Is Mrs. Smith psychic?' This, twenty-two months after my first meeting with her, was my first positive statement that she

[1] It is also said that the Order was connected with Wadham College, Oxford. If this is so the connection with Wadham must have come much later. The College was not founded until centuries after the inauguration of the Order.
[2] *Histoire de L'Inquisition au Moyen Age* by Jean Guiraud. Vol. 1, page 20.
[3] By Mr. Vicars Bell, author of the book *Little Gaddesden*.

might be thus gifted. I am sure that this possibility had occurred to me before, but I must admit that my time sense for this period is dislocated. Without my diary I could not have believed there was such a long gap before my first seeing her and her beginning to tell the story.

6

Later in December I went to tea again with Mrs. A. She was excited because she said she had discovered that I had been a Cathar. She said I must now get ready for my next incarnation. (This preparing for the next ordeal is something I emphatically disbelieve in and nothing would ever persuade me to indulge in any meditations or exercises designed for this purpose.) She told me that my best preparation for the next step was to get rid of my hatred of Roman Catholicism. There cannot be any doubt that she was justified in her strong description of my attitude towards this religion. A colleague once remarked to me that my hatred of Catholicism was strongly contaminated by fear. Hate is always tinged by fear but he meant something more specific than this. This is not to say that he had any idea that my attitude towards Catholicism was influenced by my experiences in a previous life. I feel he would have had no truck with such ideas.

I do not regard Mrs. A's remarks about my previous incarnation as in the least important. Equally one could regard them as obvious and almost inevitable. Certainly they were in the realms of conjecture. One should remember that I had not previously been interested in reincarnation before July 1962. At this date I encountered a case the symptoms of which I could not explain on any other basis. Before that date my interest in the subject was, for a psychiatrist, surprisingly small. Nevertheless, under the heading of December 20th, 1963, I find listed in my diary with my fear of Catholicism and my dislike of clericalism the fact that from childhood I have hated to destroy anything living. When I was a boy I never took birds' eggs in spite, or because of,

23

my passion for nature. Even as a so-called thoughtless child it worried me even to pick a flower and the relics of this reluctance are not dead. Most significant of all, a short period before starting my diary, I had felt a revulsion to flesh food. All this was the Cathar in me coming to the surface. The Cathars, like the Buddhists, did not approve of taking any form of life. They abstained from all flesh food, except fish.

On December 27th I went with my wife to meet the Tibetan lama who had been referred to in the letter from Falmouth. I looked forward to the visit with interest and apprehension, the latter because of an unfortunate experience I had once in the company of a group of people who were devoting themselves to a new form of enlightenment which was reputed to work with the rapidity of an efficient pain killer. (I may say that I reject totally all short cuts to salvation. I did not seek the company of these people. They practically forced themselves on me.) All I got from this experience was a fear of meeting anybody psychic or even whom I could regard as being on a higher spiritual plane than myself. I had a number of psychic friends but I had got used to them. Indeed, for the most part I had known them for years before I realised they were so constituted. I need have had no such fears about the lama. He exuded an atmosphere of ordinary good nature. Had one met him at a pit head in Derbyshire or behind a counter in Wigan one would have thought of him in such terms. He did not exude any atmosphere of piety nor did one think of him as flying over hedgerows, or even frontiers, in his spare moments. He merely emanated goodness.

Another important incident followed. My hostess, Mrs. H, handed me Fernand Niel's *Albigeois et Cathares*, a small paper back in the French series Que Sais-je. I was surprised that in an English household anybody other than a mediaeval historian would be interested in the subject. Mr. H is a public schoolmaster and his subject is physics. I think it was all of two years later that I discovered that earlier in life he had learnt Provencal and that he was interested in the poetry of the troubadours. Not many English people have learnt Provencal, which is one of the

24

forms of the Langue d'oc. This latter was formerly the language of the Midi of France and the part of Spain we now call Catalonia. The name of the region with which we are chiefly concerned, i.e. the Languedoc, is derived from the name of the language. Provencal differs somewhat from Occitan, which is the modern name for the Languedoc (both language and country) in having more Italian derivations.

To this day, only a few people in England know anything about the Cathars but it seems that it is preordained that, sooner or later, I meet all of them. Mr. H told me later that he had always assumed that my name was of Catalan origin.

The significance of this visit was twofold. Niel's simple little book was of compelling interest to me though as yet I did not know why. A good deal of what he said was elementary and basic and I knew it already. It was the old story of anything to do with Catharism having a magnetic influence on me. Mrs. Smith had not yet begun to divulge to me her revelations. The second point of importance about this visit was that there is a very considerable similarity between Catharism and Buddhism. Both believe in reincarnation, in abstention from flesh foods, though fish was allowed in Catharism, in non-resistance, that it is sinful to take the life of any living creature, even an animal etc. etc. Indeed one of the writers on Catharism, Maurice Magre, has said quite simply, and I think erroneously, that the Cathars were Buddhists.[1] Buddhism and Catharism are entwined in my sub-conscious in a system of psychic cross references. Thirdly, it is very rarely I encounter Mr. and Mrs. H without a link being supplied in some chain of psychic communication.

On the night of January 2/3, 1964, I dreamt that I was in Yorkshire and that in a field called the On, or something like it, I saw a cross on a stone and knew somehow that it had to do with the Knights Templars. The field was near the birthplace of one of the most psychic and perceptive people I have ever

[1] The reader will understand that I had not read Magre's book *Illuminés et Magiciens* at the time of which I am writing. In any case it cannot be considered a work of reference.

met. The cross had equal arms and was surrounded by a circle.

This cross is of Greek type. It is similar to the Cathar crosses and to those of Manichæen origin. (The Manichæens were also Dualists and are regarded by many as the precursors of the Cathars. The Latin Cross of the Catholic Church has one arm longer than the other.

The European origins of Catharism were in Bogomilism. This faith flourished in Bulgaria, Macedonia and Dalmatia, that is to say in areas officially under the authority of the Greek Church.

I have said that the Cross with equal arms was also affected by the Manichæens. The latter were Dualists. In a book of this nature I cannot discuss but can only define my terms of reference. Dualism is a religion, or perhaps more accurately, a religious attitude which has existed from time immemorial. It is essentially an attempt to explain the fall of man and the problem of evil. The orthodox Christian attitude leaves largely unexplained the agonising question, If God is at one and the same time all powerful and all merciful why do such appalling things happen to people and, above all, to innocent people? Dualism rejects the idea that these things are sent to try us, that God wishes to strengthen our fibre and that suffering is provided by God because

26

it is good for us. The Dualist maintains that, so far as this world is concerned, good and evil are primary and opposed energies, that there is a shifting balance between them and that more often than not evil triumphs. From this arises, depending on the degree of Dualism manifested, the idea either that this world was created by Satan or that, if not, he is essentially the ruler of it.

Now Catharism is a Christian form of Dualism. Its Manichæen precursor was to a considerable extent Christian in origin but far less so than Catharism. It follows from what one has said of the basis of Dualism that Cathar ideas as to the Incarnation of Christ were far from orthodox. The average Christian accepts that the flesh is the temple of the Spirit. To the Dualist the latter is positively imprisoned in matter. For this reason the Cathars could not accept that Christ was truly incarnate. They believed Him to be the Son of God and read His words more assiduously than did the Catholics though they interpreted them differently. But to them Christ did not exist in a human but in a spirit body. The Inquisition wrongly translated this as meaning that to the Cathars Christ was a kind of phantom. The Cathar view was in accordance with that expressed by modern spiritualists and by the adherents of Steiner. The Cathar view of Christ's existence accords also with what St. Paul meant when he spoke of the body spiritual as distinct from the body corporeal.

Dualism has existed from time immemorial. Its possible beginnings were in Zoroastrianism in Persia, though Burkitt denies that this religion was essentially Dualist. It formed the basis of the cult of Mithras during the decline of the Roman Empire and was manifested in the various gnostic creeds in the early centuries of the Christian era.

The significance of my dream of the Knights Templars is that they also were tainted with Dualism. At the time of their brutal extermination in 1307 and afterwards it was alleged against them that they had acquired noxious practices from the East. This was translated by their accusers as meaning either physical practices of an obscene nature or that they were contaminated by Islam. The truth was that in the Near and Middle East the Templars had been influenced by Dualist ideas of the perpetual war between the energies of good and evil, between, in Zoroastrian terms, the light and the darkness, the two elements being conveyed in their white and black flag.

This dream of the Greek Cross and the Templars was not the first time crosses of Greek and Manichæen design appeared in this story of the Cathars and myself. For some time previous—I cannot specify for how long but it was certainly years—I had had visions, in the process of falling asleep, of crosses of such design and of others more intricate. These visions were shortly to increase in frequency and clarity.

That morning, when I woke up after dreaming of the Templars, I thought immediately of the cult of Mithras. I could not get out of my head Kipling's Song of Mithras, which always has the power of moving me intensely. Then it came to me in a great rush of feeling, the thoughts in my mind being somehow carried on the waves of feeling, that one should not believe or try to believe, that we should only wait till one knows. My diary said, 'I see now the futility of efforts and systems and of how one must submit and wait. I understand for the first time the issue of predestination or freewill. I see that the question does not arise because time does not exist. Freewill and predestination are regarded as opposites because they are seen against the background of chronological time. But outside the prison of personality time is an illusion and therefore there is no choice and equally no predestination. There is only a timeless pattern. So one has to work as though one had freewill, but at the same time to accept the fact of what is called predestination, because all is arranged and this is one of the fundamental reconciliations of opposites. And yet all is not arranged because the pattern is neither present nor future.'

I make this quotation because the ideas of time as expressed above are at variance with the idea of eternity as prolonged duration. This has been the idea of orthodox Christianity for

28

centuries, though such concepts are changing in the present with great rapidity. From many points of view the ideas of time which I have expressed in this entry, and in previous books, fit in with those derived from the Cathar idea of how the Spirit, once emancipated from the domination of matter, exists independent of time and space.

My diary continues, 'And I saw how there has been a thread throughout all time, the Manichæes, the cult of Mithras, the Albigeois, all completely massacred, very, very completely, and among other things because of this reincarnation business.'

7

On January 6th, 1964, I went to the library and found a book on the Inquisition with a foreword by an eminent English Catholic theologian. I had been thinking of the latter with derision no more than twenty-four hours previously. I could not bring myself to take the book from the library. I felt I would be upset too much by it. I also felt an access of fear. In this book Catharism was referred to as a poisonous heresy. I have never been able to summon up courage to take this book from the library. (I have, of course, read a number of other books on Catharism written from the Catholic standpoint.)

On January 7th my wife picked up a magazine at the hairdresser's and read an article on the Order of Bonshommes at Edlington, Wiltshire. The author associated this Order with Catharism. I consider this view premature for the same reasons which I have put forward when writing of the Bonshommes at Ashridge. I wrote, however, to the author to see if she had any further information to offer. On January 17th I received a reply and discovered to my astonishment that the author of the article was one of my patients who had very recently been in hospital and under my care. On no occasion had I discussed Catharism with her.

The story takes a big leap forward on January 12th. On this

occasion I was being driven through the town during a snowfall by a member of my family. Among other things I intended to leave a note for Mrs. Smith. The message was about a hospital appointment. I cannot for the life of me think why I had not arranged this previously. I have no recollection of ever having before employed this time-wasting procedure.

Mrs. Smith herself answered the door. She admitted much later (12.2.65) that she knew I was coming. My appearance with the snow falling recalled the day she first met me in the thirteenth century. She identified me at her first appointment at out-patients, though she did not tell me this till long afterwards. The significance of the falling snow was that in my previous existence I took refuge in her father's house during a heavy snowstorm near Toulouse. Her people were humble folk and she had never seen anyone like me before, at any rate at close quarters. It appears that I belonged to the minor gentry. I apologise for this. It sounds too much like the usual reincarnation story. I am, however, no more responsible for my comfortable origins in a past life than I am for my obscure derivations in the present.

It seems that during the night I slept on the floor in the midst of the family. The so-called house was a one-roomed hovel. The girl, she was still in her teens, lay awake watching me and on one occasion stole up towards me and kissed my hand. It seemed she fell in love with me at first sight, something which has never happened to me in this incarnation.

On Sunday, January 30th, my diary begins, 'The whole thing is getting quite fantastic.' On this day my wife and I visited, for drinks before lunch, the house of a doctor friend of ours who lives in the country. During the party I got detached from the main body with a retired Senior R.A.F. Officer. He had served with distinction during the last war and had been head of a famous establishment for the training of officers in his particular Service. I mention these characteristics to show that we are not dealing with an over-suggestible, gullible and unpractical type.

30

I knew that he was a physically active man who walked a great deal and liked remote places. I asked him if he knew the Pyrenees. He said he did and described the region as very beautiful. I then hazarded my question about Montségur, the haunting mountain which I had never visited but the name of which, whenever I encountered it, gave me an indefinable stab of emotion. When I asked him this question his face sharpened and he looked at me intently. 'Yes,' he said. 'I have been there and the atmosphere was awful.'

I asked him what he meant by awful. He told me that he started to climb with his wife from the road to the peak of the mountain. Soon after he started he was seized with an inexplicable horror. He asked his wife what had happened there. He said that to him the whole place appeared to be saturated with blood and wondered if she had the same feeling. It appears that she shared his horror.

He had never before heard the word Cathar. He had no idea that, when he felt this atmosphere, he was crossing the lower slopes where two hundred Cathar Parfaits had been burnt in 1244.

He and his wife went on to the summit. When they arrived there they met a small group of people with whom my companion got into conversation. He discovered that they were the representatives of a society he described as dedicated to the memory of the Cathars.[1] From these people Air Commodore B learnt the name Cathar and the history of the place for the first time.

I said to him, 'You realise what you are saying, that you can recognise the persistence of an atmosphere after seven hundred years?'

'Of course I do,' he said. His tone was almost peremptory. 'After all, I felt it.'

It was obvious that this experience had aroused his interest in

[1] When I re-met Air Commodore B in February, 1969, he informed me that the organisation in question was the Albigensian Society. I had not previously heard of its existence.

Catharism. He described it with confidence as primitive Christianity. I am sure he was right and, what is more to the point, this is the view of many experts. He said also with great earnestness that Catharism was a dagger pointed at the heart of Roman Catholicism and for this reason it had to be exterminated. When I saw him again five years later I was surprised to learn that his interest in Catharism had not led him to read more about it. But then, would I have examined the sources as intensively as I have done if I had not met Mrs. Smith?

Shortly after this our doctor host called to us across the room. 'What are you two talking about?' I hedged and told him we were discussing something which would almost certainly be unfamiliar to him. He continued to be pressing and I told him we were discussing the Cathars. He said he had never heard of them but was rather insistent that I told him something about them. I told him that they had been active in the Pyrenees.

This touched a responsive chord. He had been with his family to the Pyrenees. He described the country as absolutely lovely but haunted. He said that on one of their long excursions he never heard a single bird. He became so preoccupied by this silence that he offered half-a-crown to the first of his four children to hear a bird singing. They concentrated hard but none heard anything.

It must have been perhaps a couple of years later when, with a greater knowledge of Catharism, I asked my doctor friend where he had stayed in the Pyrenees. He mentioned a narrow valley which leads from the valley of the Upper Ariège. It was in this area that the last remnants of the Cathars congregated towards the end of the thirteenth century. It was here that they were systematically hunted at the instigation of the Inquisition. Over a hundred were immured and left to die in the cave at Lombrives.

My intensive encounters with Catharism cannot be put down to coincidence. As a provincial doctor leading a very restricted social life, I cannot be expected to have many Cathar contacts. After all, over the whole of Britain, their number is inconsiderable. It seems that I act as a magnet to quite a number.

I should point out that the Cathar affair flared up and intensified over a period of approximately three months from the beginning of this diary to January 30th. This was one of my 'open' periods. By this I mean that all sorts of extrasensory phenomena with which I was concerned were occurring during that period. Indeed, in an essay on psychic communication, I drew largely on the period I have recently covered but in this other work I made no mention of the Cathars.

This intense psychic activity was divisible into two categories. The first one can call general and the second referred specifically to my life with the Cathars.

Under the heading of general are included the following. I encountered two striking examples of thought transference, a patient with remarkable out of the body experiences who in three days passed, from the state of infancy into which she had receded, to a rational adult state, a surprising number of patients who volunteered without questioning their acceptance of reincarnation, a remarkable piece of clairvoyance by a friend about her daughter's illness, an astonishing, sudden and scientifically inexplicable transformation in a patient whom I had previously assumed to be a psychopath or severely schizophrenic and who, in a few days' time, not only recovered but produced evidence of previous healing capacity and, finally, the day before my visit to the doctor when I met Air Commodore B, a truly remarkable case of a girl who undoubtedly 'saw' her dead grandmother.

I quote these circumstances not merely to prove that I was at that time engulfed in a considerable wave of psychic activity and that someone was acting as a transmitter.[2] I want also to make the point that, in such active periods, when so many different kinds of extra-sensory phenomena are being manifested, when one has a hunch that something is true it is as well to stick to the hunch even when the evidence is to the contrary.

[2] By this term I mean someone who incites psychic activity in predisposed sensitives in his vicinity. A transmitter, according to my definition, is usually unconscious of the function he is performing. In acting as a transmitter he himself may register no psychic experience.

By this I do not mean that, given the intuition and conflicting evidence one should opt for the former. Quite the contrary. One should go by the presented evidence but keep the hunch in mind. This is the reason why, though I rejected the hypothesis that there was a Cathar foundation at Ashridge, I still maintain that one day what I now reject will prove to be true.

8

At the end of February I went with my wife for a short holiday in the South of France. I had nothing in the way of experiences such as I recorded in my diary, except that on my way back we had dinner in Paris with a friend we had first met twenty-eight years ago. I had known previously that he was interested in Rudolf Steiner but I had not realised his interest in the Cathars. When I left next morning he made me a handsome present of reading matter for the train. It included Zoë Oldenbourg's *Le Bucher de Montsegur*. This book contains a reference to Pierre de Mazerolles, one of the central figures in my story, in fact the man in Mrs. Smith's dream. I did not know of his existence when I read this book and his name did not register with me. It is ironical that I had to go to a good deal of trouble to discover his identity and actions when he was actually mentioned in one of my early explorations of the subject. The fact that I had not previously read this popular work should prove that my knowledge of Catharism was not precocious and was built up slowly, which disposes of the possibility that Mrs. Smith obtained information from me by a process of thought-transference.

Between February and November 1964 there is not a great deal to report from the Cathar point of view. On the 28th February I received a letter from Mrs. Smith, in which she asked me if I would answer a question absolutely honestly. She wished to know whether, if she told me something known to nobody but herself, I would make a note of it and keep it in my files. I told

34

her that I did not write confidences in my notes but limited myself to the recording of symptoms. I still had to wait a considerable time for the revelation.

In this letter Mrs. Smith told me something which is of interest in revealing her make-up. She had been reading something about water divining and wanted to know more about it. Suddenly, for no logical reason, she decided that if she went out to play cards she 'might come across someone interesting'. Her hunch was right. 'I picked a middle-aged man for a partner and curiously enough he was a wart charmer. He also told me that his uncle at D—was a water diviner and well known in that district.' I think this was the first positive indication I had that Mrs. Smith was psychic, though I had suspected it beforehand. I still had to wait for the revelation.

At the end of June and the beginning of July I returned from a holiday which included the Pyrenees. At last I saw Montségur. At one stage on the journey I was convinced we would never get there, a conviction shared by my wife. The peak has a trick of hiding itself completely as one approaches it from different directions. Secondly, the car began to boil, as far as I could see for no reason. We had not mounted to any great height, our climb appeared to me to be gradual and we had driven slowly. Three things emerged from this visit. First of all, I expected to be gripped by panic when I climbed towards the peak. I was obviously very influenced by Air Commodore B's words and anticipated that I would react as he did. I felt no panic whatever. I was aware only of the beauty of the surroundings. Secondly, in my heart of hearts, after years of longing, I expected some kind of revelation. There was none for the simple reason that I was looking for it. Thirdly, I did experience a feeling of great peace when I arrived at the peak and walked in the ruins of the chateau. I felt I could have stayed there indefinitely.

Looking back on Montségur after years and after subsequent visits I am satisfied that it more than lived up to my expectations. The degree to which it now haunts me is greater than in the days before I saw it. My recollections of it serve only to heighten

35

its beauty. I have something of the same feeling also about the Corbières and the country round Fanjeaux but with these latter I have less feeling of reverence, of being in the presence of purity and sanctity, than I feel in relation to Montségur. At the same time I have more the feeling of belonging to Fanjeaux and the Corbières.

During this holiday I had the good fortune to meet Professor Nelli, the great authority on the Cathars and troubadours. His name had been given me by a friend. On the strength of this slender introduction I called on him and found him most courteous, intelligent and forthcoming. He did his best to enlighten me as to the complexities of Cathar theology, but my theological incapacity and my imperfect comprehension of spoken French proved something of a handicap.

In a letter on my return Mrs. Smith told me that once she had a sudden, blinding impulse to visit a woman living in the same town. She found her in a state of acute agitation. This woman admitted that before Mrs. Smith arrived she had contemplated suicide. She was calmed by my patient's visit. I was interested in this episode from the point of view of whether or not Mrs. Smith had the gift of healing which is perhaps the highest aspect of extra-sensory capacity. I know also the person whom she had visited. The latter had a long history of episodes of acute agitation and depression.

The most important happening at this time was a letter from Mrs. Smith on September 12th. In it she mentioned a recent holiday experience when, at St. Jean Pied de Port, she had a feeling, even at first sight, that her surroundings were familiar to her. She said that she had the same feeling of familiarity when she was staying with a French family seven years previously at Capvern in the Pyrenees. This was the occasion of her first visit to France. It is interesting and significant that the presiding hobby and interest of the father of the family was the Knights Templars. The latter and the Cathars belong to the same Dualist stream, with similar gnostic tendencies. Was something at this stage transmitted to Mrs. Smith who, as we shall see later, was a sensitive receptor of impressions not discernible by other people? Was the whole process ignited again at Capvern?

When I saw her on November 20th she enlarged on her *deja vu* experiences at St. Jean Pied de Port. Going up some steps in the town she bent down instinctively to pick up her long skirt. Glancing down she then realised that her skirt was fashionably short. She recognised the steps and, before she saw it, the street they led into. She felt she knew all the details of the interior of one of the houses in the street and that had she been able to enter it she could have verified her impression of its contents.

On the same day she met a Swiss student. She had never seen him before nor has she seen him since or corresponded with him. He said that he had seen her before but in a picture. I myself have a vague sense of familiarity with her features. Much later in our acquaintanceship she told me that my first words to her were, 'Have I seen you before?' (I do not lay much stress on this. Any doctor who has been in practice a long time is entitled to say this to a patient.)

She said that on a previous holiday she had a similar experience of familiarity with her surroundings when in Bayonne which she was visiting for the first time. I learnt later that this familiarity was associated with a feeling of gloom and horror.

On November 22nd Mrs. Smith wrote a letter amplifying what she had told me on the 20th. I cannot do better than quote from its contents. 'You have every right to be sceptical[1] and I'm not expecting you to believe me but somehow, somewhere, you are involved. Many people have this 'I've been here before' but in my case it's something more than that. There are moments when time has no significance—the past, present and future are blended. I feel I am dreaming and yet all the time I know I am wide awake.

'Perhaps I ought to tell you how you fit into this. I'm not

---

[1] She constantly over-emphasised my scepticism. I never once expressed it towards her but I was always justifiably careful in assessing the evidence from the historical point of view. Her attitude that it was inevitable that I must be sceptical derived from the fact that she never previously revealed any of her experiences to anyone, believing that nobody could possibly believe her.

being romantic—this is the way it happened at Bayonne. It's not a beautiful city. On top of the hill there is an old cathedral with a dark, ugly, oppressive interior. My first reaction was to get out of it as quickly as I could. It was here in this sombre place that I felt I was standing where I had stood before, and I'm sorry to mention this, but I had an overwhelming sense of your presence.

'I find it difficult to write about St. Jean Pied de Port, for I know the experience will seem quite ludicrous when it is written. I knew St. Jean Pied de Port as soon as we arrived there. I normally have no sense of direction but I made my way straight to the ancient gateways leading to the outer part of the city. The road leading to the fortress was very steep, as I knew it would be, and the houses were very old but quite familiar to me. I knew too that we would have to climb many steps before we reached the fortress.'

In this letter she mentioned for the first time her horror of Toulouse.[2] She had no concrete reason for not wanting to go there but was nevertheless afraid to do so. She said, 'Maybe its because I dreamt about it once. I can't remember much of the dream but I woke up terrified because I was running away from someone who was trying to force me to enter a cathedral.' She was able to name the latter. It was called St. Etienne. She said that when she heard the name of the Cathedral she did not search in any reference book to find if this were true. She said, 'The information was thrust upon me by a chance encounter I had with a French priest earlier this year. I stopped to chat with him because I thought he might have some ideas about Cathars which would be of interest to you.'[3] In the course of their conversation he offered to write to his superior in Toulouse on her behalf and also said that the Cathedral was called St. Etienne. The mention of this name must have alarmed Mrs. Smith considerably. The priest seemed to think something was wrong and

---

[2] Toulouse was the centre, the very Rome, of heresy. The fulminations of the Papacy against the Cathars involved special maledictions against the city.
[3] Mrs. Smith was always an apostle of direct action.

said to her, 'Pourquoi vous me regardez toujours comme ca?'

Mrs. Smith told me that she had a strict Catholic upbringing but had been excommunicated. She commented, referring to her excommunication, 'Perhaps my guilty conscience brought about the dream of being pushed into the Cathedral at Toulouse.' She was quite wrong here. Her dream was not a reaction of conscience but an actual memory. We shall see later that she had good reason to have a horror of Toulouse and of the Cathedral in particular.

It is interesting that I made no effort to confirm that there was a church called St. Etienne in the city, let alone that it was the name of the Cathedral. In 1965 I visited both the church of St. Sernin and also the Cathedral of St. Etienne. In spite of this I persisted in thinking that Mrs. Smith had made an error over the name of the Cathedral. I believed the latter to be called St. Sernin. It was only this year, 1969, in revising this script, that I consulted a guide book and found myself in error. Without ever going to Toulouse Mrs. Smith was more accurate than I was. This discrepancy of opinion falls into place in due course. Mrs. Smith came to grief in St. Etienne. My best friend, and possibly myself, was condemned in St. Sernin.

She also told me that she had been dreaming in French recently. Her experience of French was up to what would now be called O level but it seems to me that, though she was not engaged in any academic pursuit, she kept up her French after she left school to a greater degree than most grammar school girls.

She told me that she would like to write a novel about France but very emphatically not about the Middle Ages because she was frightened of it.[4] She added that I need not fear that she would trespass on my Cathar territory. (At this time I was far from qualifying as an expert on Catharism nor could I claim such a title now.) She also asked me if at any time I felt depressed in certain atmospheres and if at other times I felt very peaceful. She was obviously breaking the news to me gently that she was

[4] This was nothing to do with what she wrote as a schoolgirl, the existence of which was still unknown to me.

psychic. I had gathered this already. She said she felt especially peaceful at Capvern. This is in a region of the Pyrenees which was not especially affected by Catharism.

Referring back to her capacity to visit places she has not been to before and to feel them to be quite familiar, she said that she only experienced this phenomenon in France. I noticed on this particular day that her face had changed remarkably since I last saw her. To me she looked very eighteenth-century and had a hair style which was my idea of the kind of wig worn at that time.

I believe, but am not sure, that it was on November 20th that she first told me that her recurrent nightmare had ceased. My note for this day stated that I always felt she was 'one of those', i.e. psychic. More than this, my consciousness appears on this date to have accepted more fully the implications of the matter. The reference to Mrs. Smith included the cryptic note, '? Cathar'.

On the 25th November I received a letter from her. She said, 'I'm grateful that you thought the experiences of mine were interesting and not some form of madness. I still can't make up my mind if I was wise to tell you. My family used to tease me about my intuition. It amused them until I actually predicted something which affected us all, and after that they decided that there was something peculiar about me. That incident taught me to keep things to myself.' (This would explain the long interval between her letter asking if I made notes of confidences made to me and her by no means dramatic revelations of November 20th.)

I feel that during this year of psychic fermentation between November 1963 and the same month in 1964, my sense of chronological time was a bit dislocated. Had I had to write this book without my diary I would have said that Mrs. Smith had not kept me waiting such a long time before beginning her revelations. During the summer of 1964 I started to write a novel about Catharism. This was a novel of action and as much dedicated to the principles of anti-Catholicism as to admiration

40

for the broad and simple basis of the Cathar faith. At times I appeared to be living in the thirteenth century to the degree that on several occasions I began letters or notes with the date 1264 instead of 1964. I am, however, prepared to believe that this dislocation of the time sense may not have been meaningful and that, in looking back, I had merely suffered a normal and almost physiological confusion of memory.

On December 18th there is a note to the effect that I had been reading books on Catharism obtained for me by the local library. In it I wondered how much a searching and deliberate concentration on such a subject stood in the way of actual experiences.

9

The next few weeks are best divisible into two sections. What happened in this time is classifiable under two headings, firstly the episode of Mrs. Smith and Madame X, and secondly general evidence of her psychic propensities.

I will deal first with the story of Monsieur X, a foreigner of independent means and resident abroad, whose wife, now dead, had been a theosophist and interested in different esoteric subjects. Catharism had been one of her interests and she had written one or two articles on the subject in specialist papers of limited circulation. I came across one of these articles in a back number of a journal. The article contained one or two points of interest to me. I wrote to the author, asking for her sources of reference and received a kind letter from her husband explaining the circumstances and answering my questions to the best of his ability. On December 14th I had a letter from Mrs. Smith in which it transpired that she had written to Madame X on the same day as I had. While on holiday in France she had seen some reference to an article written by this lady. Later she tracked down the magazine in which this article was printed. She read it with, as we shall see, disastrous results. I should point out that at this time Mrs. Smith's knowledge of Catharism was infinitesimal and that she was only concerned with it because of my own interest in the subject.

This synchronisation of action and thought between Mrs. Smith and myself has occurred on more than one occasion. On one occasion she received a letter from me containing the identical longish sentence which she herself had written to me as her contribution to a discussion on the art of writing.

This letter of the 14th was troubled. Monsieur X had written in the most helpful and cordial manner to Mrs. Smith. She described herself as faced with a jigsaw puzzle with several pieces missing. What frightened her was that she found herself 'on the same wave length as someone else'. She was bewildered and frightened because she had an irresistible desire to write again to Monsieur X. She feared that if she did so it might in some way cause him pain. She said that she hated involving other people in trouble, all the more because at one time some friends of hers had become afraid of her. She did not want anyone else to have the same feelings about her.

On December 22nd Mrs. Smith wrote again. The tension was mounting. 'I'm beginning to get frightened. Why can I see the future so clearly and why am I getting involved with people I don't know?' Her inexplicable desire to write to Monsieur X was now countermanded by a more or less firm decision not to do so because of the peculiar impressions she was getting. Her tension was heightened by the very kindness and cordiality with which Monsieur X had expressed himself in his letter. She regarded his reaction as further and frightening evidence of her capacity to get on the same wave length as others.

In the course of an interview on December 31st she made a statement to the effect that love was an immensely creative force and that through it mankind would be bound together. The statement itself made no great impact on me. I agreed with its impeccable sentiments but found it rather trite. What did surprise me was that she was so hazy as to its derivation. She did not claim to have produced it herself. First of all she attributed it to me. I was sure beyond any possibility of doubt that I had

42

never made any such statement. I never take an elevated tone with patients. A doctor is not a preacher and in my view his approach to his patients should be passive and should not involve exhortations of this nature. After all, a consulting room is not a pulpit. At the same time I did not credit Mrs. Smith with any dubious motive in attributing this to me nor did I put it down to hysteria. I had, in relation to her statement, what I described in my diary as the 'wild idea' that the time sequence had been shuffled and that she was quoting something heard in another life. I was to discover soon that her doubts about the origin of this statement became a source of great anxiety to her.

I asked if she would let me see what she had written of what she called her novel. Mrs. Smith's writings were divisible into two categories. Firstly, there were bits and pieces taken down as they streamed in on her and as they were revealed in her dreams. These oddments included descriptions of episodes, isolated phrases or even names, recollections of life in a women's community in the Middle Ages and the memory of poems sung by a man named Roger whom she loved. The second category was the novel which was essentially the story of her life with this man. She was very sensitive and secretive about this story, as we shall see with unfortunate results. (This effort had nothing to do with the projected novel set in France but not in the Middle Ages. Her wish to write this latter book was never implemented.)

Her response to my request to see her novel was very hesitant. Finally she said she would but her doubt and reluctance were obvious.

The new year 1965 opened with a letter in which Mrs. Smith said that she would not be sending any of her manuscript. She went back on this decision later but kept to it as far as her 'novel' was concerned.[1] Again she expressed the desire to write to Monsieur X. This time she said that she could not believe she

[1] It was typical of her that she omitted to say directly in her letter that she had burnt her 'novel'. She had always a breathless interest in the immediate matter under discussion and in certain moods it would not occur to her to tell me that she had taken a destructive step which could have been of major importance in solving the riddle.

43

could hurt him in any way. Her letter also conveyed that she believed I still regarded her through the eyes of one looking for mental disorder. She was excessively sensitive on this point and somewhat unjust. From very early in my acquaintance with her I regarded her extra-sensory experiences as a true bill. She alternated between periods of frank confidence and periods of suspicion. During the latter she believed that whatever I said to the contrary I regarded her as a case and her dreams and recollections as merely symptoms. In a letter on January 10th she said, 'Never before have I confided in anyone. This was part of me I kept exclusively to myself. I vowed to myself years ago, when at the age of thirteen these inexplicable occurrences[2] started to take place, that no one should ever know. I feared, as perhaps I fear now, that I would be regarded as a crank and eventually go mad. It took me three years to decide to tell you, years of prevarication, of trying to assume an air of nonchalance etc. etc.' It was not three years. Her estimation of the flux of time was not always accurate. It was obvious from the general tone of her letter that though she had confided in me, she regretted that she felt it necessary to do so. (Her regret and her fear must have been considerable for her to have taken the step of destroying one of her manuscripts. I was not positively aware that she had done so till some days later.)

In this same letter January 10th 1965 she spoke also of 'this terrible affliction of "going out of time". I am sometimes so confused that I cannot honestly be sure if a person has just said something, or whether they will say it one day, or did so in the past'. For a person desperately anxious to be believed and taken seriously the sincerity of such a statement is convincing.

The letter of the 10th contained a most significant message. 'I did not destroy my manuscript in a moment of anger and impetuousness.' She only referred thus tangentially to this act of destruction. Such a method of reference was typical of her

[2] She is referring to her thirteenth-century experiences. Her extra-sensory gifts began to manifest themselves at the age of eleven at the onset of her so-called epileptic attacks.

unworldly and uncalculating approach to the whole matter. Even though she wished ardently to be justified and to be believed it never occurred to her to keep this manuscript as evidence of her truthfulness or because of its intense historical interest. I am convinced that it was very precious to her and something not to be shared. Her destruction of it reflects also an attitude of mind which enabled her to express surprise that wine glasses were not used, in the thirteenth century, in the house of her man Roger and that fireplaces were situated in the centre of the room. In any case that she acted as she did is to me all the more evidence of her sincerity. Anybody wishing to convince me would, at this stage, have kept the manuscript at all costs. In any case I cannot see that the novel, which as such would have to be to some extent constructed, was anything like as important as the detailed evidence she gave me in her letters, interviews and in the schoolgirl manuscript of the poems sung by Roger, evidence which, as we shall see, was in strict accordance with historical fact.

She continued writing of the destruction of the novel. 'I did so because I knew, and God knows too, that I *had* to. I resented your interest and indeed I've always actively discouraged any interest anyone shows in my writing.' And again, 'That novel was a part of me, never to be shared, never to be discussed and never to be published. Why did I write it then? I don't know. It was quite a simple story about a family living in the times of the troubadours. I knew if I did not get rid of those pages I would be guilty of plagiarism—not deliberately, but through a medium.[3] I couldn't, and still don't understand. I can't tell you exactly what I wrote because as soon as I saw it I destroyed the manuscript immediately. I couldn't get rid of it quick enough. You must understand that I hadn't looked at it for long enough, for years, in fact, since long before I saw that wretched article in the magazine.' She is referring to the fact that she had recently read the article written by the late Mdme. X, mentioned by me previously. 'The passage was to the effect that fear

[3] She is not using this description in the spiritualist sense of the word.

45

begets fear, that hate is positively creative of hate, that its effects last until eternity and until man ultimately destroys himself. I *know* these words were the same as I read in this article years after I had written them. I know because they stick in my mind and I can see now why they did so. The whole thing terrified me beyond words. I had to get rid of that book. I really had to.'

One can now see the explanation of her doubt as to the origin of her verbal statement about the creative power of love. She discovered it in her manuscript written years before she had stumbled on Madame X's article. The latter had contained an identical statement. Mrs. Smith was terrified of what she called her 'unconscious plagiarism'.

She then reverted to the theme of wanting to write to Monsieur X in order to help him. 'My life is so bound up with words yet they fail me when I need them most.' Speaking of Monsieur X she said, 'I can feel his mind reaching out towards me and I am filled with compassion, yet I am held back by a terrible fear of hurting him. Can one help a fellow being and yet hurt that person at the same time?'

IO

I saw her on December 31st. She told me that when she was very young, as far as she knew about six or seven, she was told to take the sevens out of a pack of cards and did so with the pack reversed and the backs upright. At the age of eleven she had one day a splitting headache and became unconscious. 'They thought I had an epileptic fit or something.' Next day, without realising the unusual nature of what she was doing, she told an adult acquaintance who had just received a letter and had not yet opened it what its contents would be. The news conveyed in this letter was distinctly unpleasant. Its recipient reacted badly to this act of precognition and Mrs. Smith began to regard herself as something of an outcast.

The fact that she had a headache and became unconscious

before this act of precognition is very important. These symptoms could be those of severe migraine. As I have said epilepsy was regarded as coming into the picture. Both these diseases can occur in psychic people with the capacity to slip out of time. The *déjà vu*, the 'I have been here before' phenomenon is, for example, common among epileptics.

She spoke of another recurrent dream she had had for years and which still continued. She had long hair and someone was tying it into knots and telling her that she would never get away from him. She insisted the events described in this dream occurred in Toulouse.

Once, before she was twenty, before she had ever been abroad, she was engaged to a young man who on one occasion made some disparaging remark about France. She immediately broke off her engagement.

While she was talking about the horrors of Toulouse she kept saying that she did not believe in reincarnation. It was clear that in reality she did. It is impossible to conceive of a person of her intelligence, presented with such evidence as she had accumulated for years, being other than a believer. It was obvious that acceptance of this belief was being forced on her against her will and with immense internal conflict.

She agreed with me that 'everything happens in the Pyrenees'. I had made some remark previously to the effect that so many of the heresies originated in that region and that its inhabitants seemed always to have favoured the direct rather than the theological approach to God.

It appeared that she had started her novel about the troubadours when she went to the Pyrenees in 1954. It seems evident that contact with this locality ignited her recollections. She repeated that the novel was for herself alone and was never intended for publication. I am convinced she was absolutely sincere in making this statement. She emphasised that this work had nothing to do with the Cathars. It is quite obvious that it was concerned with the Cathars but that she did not recognise them as such because the name was unfamiliar to her. She did indicate, however, that it involved the troubadours.[1] One has to recognise that her ignorance of mediaeval French history was complete as a schoolgirl and until she came to see me. It was little better even as late as the date on which I made this note (i.e. Dec. 31st, 1965). She never throughout the proceedings revealed any real interest in Catharism. She knew already its ritual and that its exponents were good and kind. Certainly, later, she skipped quite eagerly through the relevant passages of Guiraud and one or two other works, but this was motivated by her desire for final reassurance that her characters existed and that in speaking and writing of them she was not abnormal.

The most remarkable story in this interview was her account of how she was accused at school of cheating. This occurred after a terminal examination at school. Herewith is the quotation from her letter. 'I had a photographic memory and scrawled off yards of a commentary on Wordsworth word for word as in the text book. I was threatened with expulsion but escaped because I offered to do it again with a mistress present in the room to act as an invigilator.' She reproduced the whole large extract word for word as before. She was not expelled but from that day onward the photographic memory disappeared.

II

On January 9th I found myself very tired. When I lay down there was a great and rapid movement of dark purple and green bands across my field of vision. This often with me betokens psychic activity, not necessarily of a happy nature. On this day I obtained one of my most significant clues as to why Mrs. Smith had such a horror of Toulouse and of the Cathedral of St. Etienne

---

[1] One has no space here to discuss the relationship between the Cathars and Troubadours. Different authorities differ as to their degree of relationship. Two facts only need be mentioned. The houses of the nobility in which Cathar priests were received were very often those in which the troubadours were also welcomed as guests. Secondly, it is widely and convincingly held that a large proportion of the troubadour poems were religious allegories and in no sense the celebration of carnal love or of physical attraction.

in particular. I read in a monograph by Molinier that the cloister of St. Etienne was one of the places where the Inquisition met. I was not searching for this information when I borrowed this essay. I had obtained the name and title of the monograph from a biography in another book I had read and had asked for it merely to widen my knowledge of Catharism.

On January 13th there is an interesting reference to Mrs. Smith's recurring nightmare. This may have been her first *written* statement that this had ceased but I am not sure because she wrote so many letters. The extract was as follows. 'I came to you because of terrifying nightmares which strangely enough started about the same time as the other things. The nightmare was always the same. I felt there was a tall dark man standing by my right side and that he was going to hurt me. I had this nightmare frequently for about nineteen years and I don't know what it was you said or did but I've never had it since I saw you.[1] Explaining why she did not tell me straightaway that her nightmares had ceased, she went on to say, 'I don't like lying,[2] but I *had* to see you again and how could I have done so if I told you I was cured?' She then talked of how I 'cured' her of her nightmares. She obviously did not know that what occurred was not the result of any therapy but of some kind of communication and that I was merely acting as a passive instrument and need not even have been a doctor. She then revealed that from her first interview she was freed from two other symptoms. 'I used to be terrified of the dark and would never sleep without a light unless someone was with me.' Previously she had hated being left alone in the house. 'That fear left me, too, and has never returned.' Again she refers ingenuously to what she called skilful psychiatry, which simply did not come into the picture.

[1] I never 'said or did anything about' the nightmares. The reader is entitled to his own interpretation.
[2] She did not lie because I never asked her if her nightmare had ceased. I try always as far as possible to avoid asking patients about particular symptoms. What she means is that she, in her own eyes, considers that she acted dishonestly in not letting me know, after leaving a reasonable interval to see if they recurred, that she was no longer bothered by these dreams. I do not see it like this. I think she is being a bit hard on herself.

She pointed out that what she called 'sensations', by which she meant her intuitions, memories and visions, came in phases and that at such times she found it difficult to sleep and had no appetite. Also at those times she suffered from splitting headaches.

On this date she referred again to the fact that she started writing her novel in 1954. My diary points out that this date is especially significant. 1954 was also the year in which I started an illness called Menière's syndrome, which involves a disturbance of the labyrinth. I had attacks of giddiness and of being off balance accompanied by nausea. I regard such symptoms in certain individuals as being an expression of their being out of time. This kind of labyrinthine vertigo is one of the group of diseases to which sensitives are prone. My illness started within a few days of the patient's first visit to the Pyrenees. She herself was also ill at that time with a mysterious and feverish malady in which she felt awful. I know that my first attack of this wretched condition was on August 24th, 1954. I wished Mrs. Smith had been able to tell me more accurately the date of her holiday in the Pyrenees. When one is dealing with such people the more there is synchronisation of time across distance the more emphatic the evidence for one or other of the varieties of psychic communication.

I discovered a tiny reference to Monsieur X's wife in a small paper of esoteric inclination. It appears that she died in 1954.

On the night of January 14th I had, seemingly beneath my eyelids, the procession of vivid and actively passing colours I have mentioned previously. I then saw two 'brilliantly silver, shining, moving open flowers with many petals'. This glut of adjectives is how I described it in my diary, always written with great rapidity. Students of oriental literature will not fail to notice that my experience is a visual symbolism of the opening of the lotus flower associated with increasing enlightenment. My knowledge of symbolism is negligible but the fact that these visions should appear at this time is significant.

The night following this vision I dreamt of Mrs. G., the first patient who seriously directed my thoughts towards reincarnation. In it she had injured her right leg and I was helping her down a hill. Two nights later I dreamt of her again. She was coming to me down a long flight of steps in a high village. My note says, 'Obviously one thinks now of France.' There may have been some connection here with Mrs. Smith's experience at St. Jean Pied de Port. These latter observations are mere supposition. What is worth noting is that I should have dreamt twice in three nights about Mrs. G., for the simple reason that, until just before this period, I very seldom dreamt of people I knew. (It was not that I knew Mrs. G. well. In all I had four appointments with her.) If I dreamt of humans at all I did not, at this time, picture them as specific and nameable entities. I raise the question of these dreams because, in a story like this, one can never be sure who initiated the psychic chain in which one finds oneself neatly entangled.

12

On January 25th I was busy sorting into chapters a novel I had written about the Cathars. My diary recorded, 'I am always writing 1200 for 1900. Noted this duly, went to write down another date, did the same thing again, told Mary[1] when she returned home what I kept doing, then afterwards made another note and did the same thing again!'

On January 30th the figures under my eyes when I was lying down were as follows:

1.

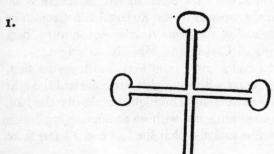

[1] My wife.

Later the symbol changed to:

2.

and later to:

3.

This is to say that in the cross shown on diagram 3 a bright shining point appeared at the intersection of what was the original cross before that of St. Andrew added itself.

The area of all the crosses are equal in length. There is no long vertical arm to the cross as in the Roman Latin Cross. The protuberances at the end of the arms are also significant. These crosses resemble those of Cathar and Manichæen origin.

On February 2nd I had a letter from Mrs. Smith saying that, as she had gone three years without nightmares, she had thought of not keeping her appointment. The night previously she had, however, awakened screaming, but with no accompanying dream she could remember. She said also that she had had a letter from

52

Monsieur X in which he had asked about her family names. 'I can't tell him much about my family because my father and all his relatives are dead. I only know that my grandfather was born at a place called Ashridge *in Kent*.' (The italics are mine. This is very important. Ashridge is not in Kent but in Hertfordshire.) By turning back these pages the reader can see that Ashridge is the place where this story of Catharism begins.[2] This is also further testimony that Mrs. Smith had no considerable book knowledge to help her and was not a type to rig the evidence.

Her grandmother, after her parents died, was sent to a convent and brought up by Irish nuns. While Mrs. Smith's Catholic ancestry is indisputable, she wrote that she had only recently realised that her very close friends have always had one thing in common. All of them were brought up as Roman Catholics and rejected the faith. If Mrs. Smith appears to attract heretics my family history is quite liberally sprinkled with contact with Roman Catholics. In this life I only escaped being Catholic by a hair's breadth. My grandfather fell in love with a Catholic girl but refused to marry her unless she abandoned her faith. I have also received a great deal of help and loyalty from Catholics. Perhaps all this means I must learn to forgive them.

13

A short note from Mrs. Smith dated February 4th raises the tension of the story. The main characters and the scenes of their actions are now being introduced. She asks me if I have heard the name Fabrissa. Was it a person or a place? During these next few days there was a considerable amount of psychic activity in the way of people pouring precognitive dreams and such like at me. On February 12th I had a further letter from Mrs. Smith.

[2] As I read over these pages it seems strange that I did not revisit Ashridge for thirty-six years. Nobody can accuse me of a persistent and demanding obsession with the subject of Catharism.

In this is a fuller and more conscious and verbal acceptance of reincarnation. She must have believed in it previously. It is remarkable how much energy she must have wasted on her rearguard action. She referred to the morning when I called at her house. Speaking of the occasion she said, 'I knew you would come. It was a Sunday and it was snowing, and I remembered that years ago you called on us on the Sabbath during a heavy snowstorm. I was convinced it would happen again, and I got into a terrible panic when you *did* call on us. I can't ever remember the reason for your visit—.' (As I have said, no more can I.)

'I think I was living just outside Toulouse, or may be in Toulouse itself, when you came to my house years ago in that snowstorm. We were a very poor family but you were of noble birth. I fell in love with you then, and my father said I must never meet you again—you were not of our class and what was more important to him, you were not of our faith. We were Roman Catholics. I refused to be parted from you, and was eventually excommunicated. I went to live with you. We weren't married. You told me that if anything should happen to you I must go to Fabrissa. That's why I asked you about that name. It could be a place, or it could be a person. I've never found out. I remember, and I wish I didn't, the anguish of losing you and the terrible loneliness I felt without you.'

She then continued this letter with such phrases as, 'The things I've said in this letter sound quite mad, but I can be sensible about it all. It is not necessary for you to feel sorry for me now that you know all the facts.' (The latter was an understatement. She had a great deal more to tell me.) She asked whether in view of what she had told me she should keep her next date at the hospital. 'I want also to be cured of these screaming attacks but not if it's going to bother you.' Her basic recurrent nightmare had gone but at times she still woke up screaming but without any accompanying dream. She also implored me to secrecy about her confidences. Later, as she learned to accept her make-up, she gave me permission to write up the story if it was of any value to anybody. It is.

Looking back on my notes for February 23rd I see that I had a dream that I was *not* going back to University and felt an immense relief. Quite often in recent years I have had this dream that I am back at University. It has replaced the one in which I am doing an examination on the morrow and haven't opened or sometimes even bought a book on the subject. The not going back to University dream now includes a relieved and happy realisation that I have a medical degree and therefore there is no point in going up for further examinations which I will fail anyhow. Previously I have not bothered much about the significance of this insecurity dream but now it appears to be as plain as a pikestaff. I take it as indicating that I need no longer bother myself too much with the materialistic and scientific aspects of medicine. In short I can follow my own inclinations and be a real doctor. I have enough qualifications to justify my following my intuitions and to allow myself to be directed by the prevailing wind bearing down upon me.

On February 26th Mrs. Smith said that the first time she saw me she felt she recognised me after the passage of centuries. It was on this date that she pointed out that my first words to her were, 'Have I seen you before?' I myself had no such memories. The recollection of my going to her house near Toulouse in the snowstorm came sometimes in dreams and sometimes when she was at her daily chores such as ironing. She said with great conviction that if she tried to remember nothing happened. I am sure that this would be my own experience were I thus gifted.

It transpired that the dream about being dragged out of a church at Toulouse started since she met me. She cried out Tolosa in the dream. This was the name for Toulouse in the Langue d'oc. The name St. Etienne came to her on waking from her dream. I am sure that her nocturnal screamings related to her experience in Toulouse and had nothing to do with her basic recurrent and now banished nightmare. Her general dread of Toulouse, as apart from the Church of St. Etienne, dates from 1954. During her holiday in France that year somebody

55

mentioned Toulouse and she was inexplicably seized with terror. Her fear of this city began long after her original nightmare was well established. The explanation of her dread of Toulouse will be seen later to be quite simple.

Mrs. Smith said that she had a theory that you cannot look forward unless you can look back. The looking forward is impossible unless you have looked back for a pattern. She wondered if the woman who had foretold the assassination of President Kennedy had had a backward look at the assassination of President McKinley in 1867.

14

On February 28th I had a horrible dream. I felt a presence to the right of me. I heard a voice in the air but I did not know what it was saying. When I awoke there was still a presence there and the air seemed thicker and rather palpitating. I was so frightened I went to look for the cat to keep me company. On March 1st I had an apocalyptic dream of standing on a plateau with a mountain on my right. The top blew off the mountain. Then, straight ahead, there were other mountains. As I watched these latter they were levelled and 'a stream of fire and lava flowed towards me in a great, wide wave. It came to me that if I moved to the left I would be saved'.[1]

I do not know if these obvious cosmic dreams are connected with the fact that next day, March 1st, Mrs. Smith wrote me a letter which drew my attention to my previous visit to this planet. I received on this day the first evidence of my existence in the thirteenth century.

In this letter she asked me if she had 'told me about him'. (She is a very intelligent woman with a very good memory but there is sometimes some shuttling of time experience when she is dealing with her own inner life. She had at any rate told me that he came to their home in Toulouse.) 'I talk of Roger in my

[1] Extract from my diary.

56

sleep.' This was the first time she had mentioned by name the man she had loved. 'I call out for him if I have a terrifying dream.' She said that in the house at Toulouse she had vague memories of another woman living there. The house she refers to here is not her home. It is one in which she lived with Roger.

In the course of this month Mrs. Smith wrote one or two letters in which she said she had no further need for appointments. It was obvious that she still passed through periods during which she regretted confiding in me. This is not surprising considering she had conducted a private war with herself for twenty years, fighting down constantly her idea that she was mad or bad and that people would think her one or the other if they knew the facts about her.

She came, however, to an appointment on March 30th. In her sleep she had been calling frequently for Roger. She was telling Roger how to get out of Toulouse by going through the woods. (Toulouse suffered terribly during the Albigensian wars.) In her dream she was so worried about Roger's safety that her husband had to quieten her by saying that he himself was Roger and that he was there beside her.

She said that in one dream she had shouted out about the crypt at St. Etienne at Toulouse. It is possible that prisoners were detained in the crypt of the Cathedral before being interrogated in the cloister. Or it may well be that torture was applied in the greater seclusion of the crypt. In any case, my surmise that Mrs. Smith had had an agonising experience in the cathedral of St. Etienne at Toulouse proved, as will be seen later, to be essentially accurate.

This patient had patches in which she wrote a great number of letters. There cannot be any doubt that this helped to clarify the situation for her. It certainly did so for me. It is only by reading her letters and comparing them with my diary that I can see how slowly, sometimes not so slowly, and very surely the puzzle began to fit into place. In all my correspondence with her I did no more than reassure her that her recollections were not symptoms of insanity and supply her with what information I could as to the questions she raised. This involved, on my part, a fair amount of study. I never in any sense 'treated' her in writing.

During the early part of April her letters were charged with regret that already she had said so much and she reverted to the theme that it would have been better had she been regarded as a psychiatric case. The whole business was painful to her and the process of revelation may well have been excruciating. In addition the phases in which she felt low, thwarted and resentful may have preceded episodes of further enlightenment. Frustration and depression before revelation is commonplace on the psychic plane and most creative artists have had this experience. Anyway, in a letter on April 15th there was a further great step forward.

'A few months ago I was reading a newspaper and talking about nothing in particular when all of a sudden I knew the identity of the man who had frightened me for so long. He had never really intended to hurt me at all. I was afraid because I was asleep (on the floor) and he was standing by my side when I awoke. I thought he had come to tell me that something terrible had happened to Roger. This man was a strange character. He had murdered someone and wasn't sorry about it. He looked quite wild and laughed and said he was glad.'

This description corresponds exactly with the character and behaviour of a certain Pierre de Mazerolles. The evidence for his character and behaviour is derived from the testimony of one of his confrères, Imbert de Salas, Serjeant at Arms, before the Inquisition at Carcassonne.[2] Pierre's character is described later in greater detail by Mrs. Smith. The further details she provides correspond with still greater exactitude with those mentioned by Imbert de Salas. (There is no question of thought transference here. I did not come across the testimony of Imbert de Salas till much later in the proceedings.) In addition, as we shall see later, the description of Pierre de Mazerolles also corresponds with uncanny accuracy to that revealed in two nightmares I had at a later date. The point at issue is that de Mazerolles had taken

[2] Doat t.xxiv, p. 172.

part in a murder, that he was elated at having done so, that the murder was an historical event and that he returned to boast of his exploits and possibly to be reassured about them. Mrs. Smith's dream is a memory of this gentleman's return from the killing.

Her letter continued. 'Roger wasn't involved in this brutal murder but I didn't want to be told about it and I was shocked and afraid. This man tried to kiss me and I screamed and he laughed at me.' In my Cathar novel there is a character who was coldly exhilarated by killing and who tried to kiss the sweetheart of the central character. I was writing this novel before I knew anything of Pierre de Mazerolles.

There is then a heart cry in the letter in which the patient obviously wishes to escape from a painful reality. 'How can anyone sane think up such fantastic stories? What sort of mother can I be to my children?' And then immediately, 'Something peculiar happened a short while ago. My younger daughter was restless in the night and when I went to her bedroom I swear she was speaking French and yet she knows only a few words. I told her in French to go sleep and she settled down. I must have imagined all this too. She has never been taught any French—she is only seven years old.'

'I'm not going to France any more. It only makes me worse.' She said that her husband had told her that when, recently, she had cried out for Roger in her sleep she had pronounced the name French fashion.

At this stage the nearer the patient got to seeing the pattern of the whole thing the more she was subject to rapid fluctuations of mood in some of which she described herself as mad and accused me of believing the same. These patches were followed by grateful letters in which she said she was much more peaceful and was grateful to me for believing what she said and for reassuring her as to her sanity.

Somewhere about April 17th I received a short note. 'If when you are in France you should meet Fabrissa, Roger, Pierre de Mazerolles or any of this mad crowd, tell them to go to hell.

They'll be better off there than in my imagination.' But they did not exist in her imagination. You can read about them in various depositions made to the Inquisition.

On April 22nd I went to Cumberland. Before setting off I was given one or two magazines, *Plaisirs de France*, by a French friend, a Catholic, for light holiday reading. I was surprised to find in one of them a not very profound article on Catharism. I was still more surprised to see a picture of Professor Nelli. He was standing at the door of some kind of institution with a woman dressed in religious habit. The institution was a house in Fanjeaux with Cathar connections. I am not sure whether the article mentioned that the house had previously belonged to the Durfort family. At any rate I had no knowledge at that time that I and the characters with whom I was connected in the thirteenth century either belonged, were married into, or closely connected with this family.

15

I received a letter dated April 25th which gave a further picture of Mrs. Smith's psychic capacities. One cannot encounter far memory without other psychic attributes. 'The whole business seemed to start with that incident over my friend's letter.' (The reader may remember that, when she was eleven, Mrs. Smith told an acquaintance what was in a letter before the recipient had opened it.) 'There was more to it than that. I had never met her young man at the time but I knew that he wouldn't marry her. Unfortunately I told her so, and afterwards I felt strangely afraid when the discussions about the wedding were taking place.' When Mrs. Smith's predictions came true there was naturally an uproar and her acquaintance treated her as though she were responsible. 'After that, if I had any ideas about future events, I didn't say a word.'

'The fact that I predicted my father's death isn't very surprising. He had been in and out of hospital for years. He was very ill and no one expected him to live as long as he did. The strange thing about his death was that I knew beforehand the exact time he died, although oddly enough it didn't worry me unduly that I should have known this detail.[1] It wasn't the first time I had known someone was going to die.'

She then referred to the time when she was considered epileptic, on the strength of her three attacks of unconsciousness. The trouble was that, when she found that she was doing what she called a 'mind-reading act' she thought that she was, to use her own words, 'going a bit queer because I was an epileptic. I had also vague ideas in my mind about having lived before'. She wondered if such ideas were symptoms of epilepsy but it did not appear that they were. 'I had the choice, it seemed, of being an epileptic or a lunatic.'

She then said how she had involved herself in a quarrel about nine years previous to writing. 'The trouble is I am not very knowledgeable about time. I'm never sure if I've already been told something or will be told about it later, I casually asked someone how she felt about being a grandmother.' The lady in question had not realised that she was qualifying for this title. She was furious with her son and his wife because they had not told her that her first grandchild was expected. The father was 'terribly angry with me'. Mrs. Smith continued, 'I tried to explain that I thought his wife had already told me that she was pregnant and he replied that I was psychic. He said it with such venom that I felt I was a leper.'

Speaking of me she said, 'I didn't know if you were naturally remote and a little hostile, or if this was how psychiatrists behaved towards their patients. I wasn't helped much by the fact that I kept mixing you up with who you were and who you are now.' This accounts for the fluctuating tone of her letters in which gratitude for reassurance and reluctance at having spoken alternate with one another.

On May 1st I had a dream which is of considerable significance.

[1] Mrs. Smith says, 'oddly enough'. In actual fact nervous patients tend to take the fulfilment of such premonitions with remarkable serenity.

I dreamt I was in the basement of a house with a laughing and sardonic individual. He was in a strange mood, a mixture of the macabre and the burlesque. I believed that he was asking me to collaborate in the production of a story or dream. In this he suggested the liquidation of some other individual. It was only later in the dream that I realised that this creature was not play-acting but serious and in my dream I had a terrible feeling of horror and anguish. This dream ties up with Mrs. Smith's description of the man who used to appear in her dream and whom she described as having committed a murder and thinking it funny. In addition Roger was not involved in this episode and as a practising Cathar must have been horrified by it. It seems that in my dream I was reflecting Roger's attitude. One can say that my nightmare was instigated by having heard the details of Mrs. Smith's. This is certainly the most reasonable explanation. At the same time it should be remembered that my own life-long nightmare of a man entering my room ceased within some months of my first meeting Mrs. Smith. In any case, however much my dream was imposed by Mrs. Smith's, the fact remains that it, too, depicts the return of Pierre de Mazerolles from his murderous foray.

In an undated letter, I think some time in April, she said how she hated this 'shuttling backwards and forwards in time. It has always landed me in trouble, caused me great unhappiness, and I hate it'. She described how one of her father's friends spent his last leave with her family before he went back on active service. He was later torpedoed and went down with his ship. 'He was the same as me, I realise that now. We never said anything, but he knew.[2] He told me I must never worry. How I wish that man hadn't been killed. I had so many unanswered questions in my mind, so much that I wanted to ask him, and now I need his shoulder to cry on.' But she goes on to say, 'I can't believe this thing is only evil.' It was as though there still lingered in her mind a feeling of guilt about her potentialities.

[2] This makes perfect sense. People on this wave length can recognise each other without speaking.

16

Early in May my wife and I went to France. It was during this holiday that I visited Professor Nelli for the second time and heard his reasons, identical with my own, for starting a diary.

We also visited an institution at Fanjeaux, the chapter house of which was formerly the residence of the Durfort family and which is now a home for deprived girls. It was inevitable that we were taken round by the Superior whose photograph I had seen at Scale Hill in Cumberland when reading *Plaisirs de France*. She herself referred spontaneously to Professor Nelli's visit. I enjoyed looking round the house. I must say I had no special feeling of recollection. As we shall see later, Roger must have been in this house on innumerable occasions.[1] Fanjeaux was the very heart of Catharism in this area and the noble heretical families were greatly intermarried. Roger was the grandson of the famous troubadour, Guillaume de Durfort. The latter was the owner of this house in Fanjeaux.

What was of more interest was that on our first afternoon en route for Carcassonne, and before we had stayed a night there, I was sitting in the car, not driving and in that heavy, semi-hypnotic state which comes when you have been hours in a car in summer weather and have become torpid and unobserving. All at once, some miles out of Carcassonne, I saw the name Mazerolles on a signpost. This gave me a thrill. I had previously looked for this place on the map. I had hitherto failed to find it because I had looked for it always in the neighbourhood of Toulouse. To date Mrs. Smith's narrative had been centred for the most part on that town.

When we visited the place later I had the same feeling as we had at Montségur. I felt we would never get there. The name seemed, in a manner unusual in France, to disappear from the signposts. I thought the country on the way to Mazerolles was

[1] He may even have been born in it.

63

beautiful. Again I had no feelings of recollection about the place itself.

On May 16th there is a note in my diary to the effect that 'this is the first holiday on which I have been "open"'. This statement should be qualified considerably. What I mean is the first holiday since I started to take notice of these things, say, a matter of four years. There were a few examples of my wife and I thinking the same things at the same time. There was the business of seeing Mazerolles on the signposts. Had I not looked up at that moment I would never have seen it. I would have gone on thinking it in the neighbourhood of Toulouse or as entirely disappeared.

On the same day I met Monsieur Déodat Roché, one of the most important of the modern interpreters of Catharism and who has been referred to, with deplorable sensationalism and inaccuracy, as the Pope of Catharism. I had from him a great impression of integrity and asceticism. My wife was similarly impressed. That we should have had this impression is important because I have come to believe that Catharism is of utterly vital importance in this age of materialism. One does not look for a revival of Catharism. You cannot live creatively outside the idiom of your age. The great majority of modern students of Catharism cannot be said to be exponents of it. One has no wish to foist a twelfth- and thirteenth-century conception on the twentieth century. But in contemplating Catharism one is not investigating an interesting and noble heresy but returning to primitive Christianity. It is for this reason that it was comforting to meet an exponent of Catharism who emanated goodness and who was described, on a subsequent visit, by a Catholic friend of mature years and after an instant's observation as the incarnation of all that was good.

Again, on May 10th, I had a repeat dream at Pau of taking part in some real and terrifying drama which I had felt at first to be 'theatre'. I felt that this was once again the shadow cast by Pierre de Mazerolles.

During May there was for some time a lull. Mrs. Smith's

letters betoken greater peace of mind. Nothing very much happened to me. On the 16th June I recalled in my diary how, in the past, I had been at times sensitive about my uncommon name. I wondered if it marked me out in some way as different. In the south-west of France, in the Midi generally, names beginning with Guir are very common indeed. The 'ham' obviously originated as an Anglo-Saxon corruption of 'an' or 'on'. In the entry in my diary I wondered whether my fear about my name and my fear of Catholicism stemmed from the same source. One of the punishments inflicted on the Albigeois was that they were forced to wear a yellow cross on their clothes as a badge of infamy. In modern times Jews were treated by the Germans with identical childish malevolence.

The day afterwards my second daughter told me that frequently in her dreams she saw a sunny white square with houses. She described the scene as being like in Spain. She knows this latter country quite well but is almost totally unfamiliar with the south-west of France. Off and on for years I had visions, when falling asleep, of people with mediaeval faces dancing in a semi-clownish manner in a sunny square. My daughter was conceived in Nimes. Somewhere back in my mind is a haunting recollection of a quarry by a sunlit road. I have always thought of this place as in the neighbourhood of Nimes. I do not think this Provencal connection comes in the Cathar story. It may well have to do with another incarnation.

On July 12th I received a letter from Mrs. Smith. She had read a book of mine dealing to some extent with extra-sensory perception. It seemed that it had helped her because she could see that what I had written in this book tallied with the verbal and written reassurances I had given her. She said, 'You are obviously genuinely interested in this subject and I wouldn't like to mislead you into believing that I'm always right. Sometimes facts become badly distorted.' She then quoted the following example. 'Early this year I dreamt that a woman I used to work with, a Gwendoline Ellen Grenville, had died. In my dream I saw the announcement in the paper. A few days afterwards

65

there was a death announcement concerning Gwendoline Ellen Granville, with whom I had no connection whatsoever. The woman I know is still very much alive. I don't know why some facts get distorted like this, but they often do.' I equally cannot explain such distortions but they do occur, and the fact that Mrs. Smith admits to such errors is further evidence of her honesty.

In the same letter she said that she once took part in an extra-sensory experiment in the form of a guessing game. Those taking part were asked to guess the nature of objects in a box. She tried and was hopelessly wrong. People of her type come out badly in E.S.P. experiments. This is because their psychism results from the temporary abnegation of their human ego. The psyche, in fact, takes over. In E.S.P. experiments the human ego is exercising itself in competition with other egoes. True-bill psychics are for the most part useless at forecasting Derby winners. If such qualities are included in their armoury it is often to their detriment.

On August 17th I had another letter. Mrs. Smith had been visiting friends in Scotland. She felt sure she was improved because something happened there which, a few months earlier, would have worried her a great deal. She had not been in the house long before she noticed in the bookcase the book of mine to which I have referred in the last paragraph but one. She wrote, 'My friend nearly bowled me over by remarking that she was enjoying the book I had recommended. I know I am inclined to be forgetful but I am absolutely certain that I have never recommended this book to her or anyone else, especially as I had no idea at this point what her views on such a subject would be.'

In the same letter she reverted to the theme of her original nightmare. This had been of such intensity that she would never stay in guest houses or hotels because of it. For the first time she raised no objection to my confirming the facts from her husband.

She then expressed an idea she had mentioned on a previous occasion. This was that she should visit Toulouse alone. She said, 'I'm not anxious to search for facts but I am sometimes frustrated because my dreams end at the same point every time. It's like reading a book and finding that the author hasn't written the last chapter. I'd like to know if I ever went to Fabrissa and if this is a person or a place.' (I had by this time satisfied myself that Fabrissa was a person.) 'I'd be interested to know how I managed to carry the money I had to take there because the sack seemed to contain all coins.' Later in this story she explains the circumstances in which she was given the sack of coins. Her statement reveals once again that what she had discovered was directly and not by study. She did not know that paper money was not in use in the Middle Ages.

17

On September 13th Mrs. Smith went further back into her past. At the age of four or five she was given a very small woolly dog called Roger. She has always hated the name Roger. At the age of eleven she nearly died from peritonitis. It was believed she would not last the night and her parents were sent for. She kept calling for Roger during the night.

It was during this illness, when her life was being despaired of, that the Last Sacrament was brought to her. At this time she was still a practising Catholic. When she saw the priest and the accompanying nuns she screamed with terror. She refused to accept the Last Sacrament. It is quite possible to attribute this to the fears of a delirious child, but does it tie up with her recollection of her Cathar past and her consequent horror of Catholicism? I think it does. It should be emphasised that the Cathars rejected the sacraments of the Roman Church. Perhaps her calling out for her woolly dog Roger provided a verbal link with the thirteenth century. In any case her reaction on seeing the priest and nuns was so extreme that the doctor in charge, a most liberal and understanding man, indicated firmly that the child's terror was such that on no account must the priest and the nuns be permitted to visit her again during her illness.

In another dream she had there was always an older woman in the big house where she was living with Roger. She did not know her identity but recollected that she was always sympathetic and helpful. It came to her in a dream that the woman's name was Alice. Next day in order to remember it she wrote this name down on a piece of paper. Having done so she reflected how stupid it was to write down, in order to memorise, a name which, after all, was that of her own mother. She went to tear up the piece of paper and then found that she had spelt the name Alaïs. I noted in my diary on this date that it was imperative that I write to Professor Nelli. I subsequently did so and found that Alaïs was a girl's name common in the Languedoc in the thirteenth century and that there were other alternative methods of spelling such as Helis. The discovery of this name proved subsequently to be of cardinal importance in identifying the principal figures in this localised version of the Cathar tragedy. It is fascinating to think that one can read the deposition made by Mrs. Smith's Alaïs to the agents of the Inquisition on August 5th, 1243.

Mrs. Smith spoke of her recurring dream in which she was setting off on a journey carrying money. She added that in this dream she is going off to another woman. At this stage in the proceedings I assumed the other woman to be Fabrissa. While she was actually talking to me she wondered if Fabrissa was the mother of Pierre de Mazerolles. This conjecture was wrong but she was right in that they were intimately related. Fabrissa was, in fact, his aunt.

She described two houses, that of her family and a big house in which she lived later. She was diffident about saying that in her own house the fire was in the centre of the room. She was unaware that this was common in the Middle Ages and that the smoke went through a hole in the roof above the fire.

She admitted that she was afraid of the idea of being a Cathar. She said that when Roger died seven hundred years ago she tried to kill herself. She hesitated a good deal before saying this and

68

was still more embarrassed when she added that she had tried to do so by starvation. She was still haunted by the fear of being thought mad or eccentric. She had had this recollection for years in her dream.

What is important in this statement is that death by starvation is said to have been practised by the Cathars. As a positive act of suicide it was rare and was positively advocated by only one Parfait, Pierre Autier, in the desperate decline of Catharism towards the end of the thirteenth century and then only in the area of the Upper Ariège. It was probably more common practice for people who had received the Cathar Sacrament, the Consolamentum, on their deathbeds to abstain from taking nourishment in order not to prolong life unduly. This particular practice was called the Endura. Its importance and the frequency of its occurrence have been greatly exaggerated by Catholic critics of Catharism.

The latest evidence produced by Monsieur Duvernoy indicates that the Endura was merely a name given to one of the prescribed periods of fasting and was not specifically related to death by starvation. Monsieur Duvernoy has the support of Mrs. Smith's direct remembrance of the thirteenth century. In a letter dated April 5th, 1966, she wrote, 'Over the years their (i.e. the Cathars') doctrines and philosophy of life have been twisted out of recognition. They were not fanatics about fasting and emphatically did not approve over enthusiasm for self-starvation.'

The fact that Mrs. Smith wished to die by starvation does not prove that such intentions were common among Cathars.

She admitted that the manuscript she had torn up and which she called the novel was the story of her life with Roger. On the same afternoon I had a strange experience which I will not describe in detail because it is written elsewhere. I was walking down the street when there came to my mind the picture of old men praying or singing hymns in a dark and gaunt building. I knew that this was in France and that these people were victims of persecution. I fell down heavily and without warning. In the course of this same walk of not half a mile I had this vision

69

three times and on each occasion I fell or stumbled. I connect these three episodes in the afternoon with my interview with Mrs. Smith in the morning. My time sense was dislocated by the latter. Loss of balance is usually regarded as being due to loss of balance in space. So it is, in its expression, but in its causation it can be due also to loss of balance in time, which is what happened this particular afternoon.

18

I received a letter dated September 14th in which Mrs. Smith, commenting on her reaction when she first read St. Paul's words on spiritual gifts, said, 'That anyone should be instructed to, and wish to, aim at such gifts was beyond my comprehension. I never aimed for them, and I didn't want them either. To be absolutely honest I don't think I really want them now, in fact I'm sure I'd turn them down flat if I could be given the choice to have or to have not,' she said, 'Reincarnation is a subject I believe in, seldom talk about and never read about. All the ideas people have about returning in the world as a horse, a cow or such like are ridiculous. The spirit is born, lives and never dies.' She then goes on to say that we can never die because we are born out of love which is creative but cannot be created by man at will. 'The secret lies in the fact that man cannot control, wish upon himself or destroy spiritual love, for God is love.'

In this letter she says she has been sorting out the bit about Fabrissa. She says now she is sure she was a woman and a relative of sorts of this murderer de Mazerolles (Pierre de Mazerolles). 'I'm glad I don't know more about him after the way he terrified me for years.' I myself was to find much more about him in the course of my investigations.

She said that now she wished that she had not burnt her novel. She said she wrote it in phases and that at times she didn't touch it for months. This is easy to understand. She obviously wrote in her psychic phases when impressions were pouring in on her. 'There wasn't much to it. No publisher would have looked at it. I felt it belonged to me alone and publication was not my intention.' Its construction was obviously fragmentary in that she was merely putting down episodes and memories as they came to her.

'The story was very simple really. The characters were my dream characters. The man spent a lot of time going around teaching people and talking to them. Activities like that suited me. Through him I wrote page after page of my religious beliefs, hopes and fears. All very arty and cultured. The sort of book I can't really cope with. It's funny that I should have written in a style that isn't really mine at all.[1] When I saw what I'd written years ago and saw how it resembled the writing in that article I was horrified and couldn't get rid of that manuscript quickly enough.' She is referring to the extracts from her novel which so resemble those written by Monsieur X's wife. People with more knowledge of the psychic than I will know to what extent she was in contact with the deceased lady.

'That novel was a hopeless failure from the start anyway. One couldn't write anything of that sort without methodically collecting and sifting through facts and reading mountains of history books on the period in question. At that stage I didn't want to know anything about the Middle Ages, which on the face of it didn't seem a bit logical. The girl in this novel was very young, became pregnant and lost the child and desperately wanted another and never did. When her lover died she decided to commit suicide by fasting, was persuaded not to, and made her way to some other town. En route she went through a city where a violent, bloody and awful battle was raging, and the silly young fool joined in by throwing stones and hurling abuse.'

In the siege of Toulouse women are recorded as taking part in the battle. It is traditional that Simon de Montfort, the leader of the Crusade against the Albigensians, was killed by a stone pro-

---

[1] In my view Mrs. Smith writes in her letters an extraordinarily good, lucid and unpretentious style. One should bear in mind that it is clear that she writes very rapidly.

pelled by a woman. Tradition has it also that he died not far from the Cathedral of St. Etienne which has proved such a horror to Mrs. Smith. I do not think Mrs. Smith is referring to the siege of Toulouse. There were two sieges of Fanjeaux and one of Montréal.[2] As we shall see later, in these towns the influence of Roger's family and those to whom it was connected by marriage was paramount. I mention Toulouse merely because I have definitely read that women played a part in the defence of the city. What happened at Toulouse could also have been enacted at Fanjeaux and Montréal.

'She, together with many others, was taken to a Cathedral[3] for the part she had taken in this battle, but bribed her captors with money and managed to escape. She ran from the cathedral "as though the very devil were after her", and at that part I'll leave you in mid air because that's as far as I got and I never got any further.'

She ended her letter as follows. 'It's a colossal relief to know you don't think I'm an epileptic. Thank you so much for telling me.'

On September 20th I had more detailed evidence of the synchronisation between my Meniére's illness and Mrs. Smith's first visit to the Pyrenees. My illness began on August 24th, 1954. By hunting up a past diary she found that, while in the Pyrenees, she was sick and with a high temperature on August 20th.

Following an interview with Mrs. Smith I had a letter dated September 20th. (At this time Mrs. Smith almost invariably

[2] In showing me round Toulouse early in October 1969 Monsieur Duvernoy pointed out the place where, by tradition, de Montfort met his death, and said that the site indicated must be pretty accurately located. He also said that there may well be truth in the contention that the leader of the Crusade was killed by a woman because it was an established fact that women worked the stone-throwing engines of war at the siege of Montréal. Mrs. Smith may well have been active in this last event. Later she gives a graphic description of the part she played in what must have been the siege of Fanjeaux.

[3] This must have been the Cathedral of St. Etienne in Toulouse. Even if she took part in fighting at Fanjeaux and Montréal that is most emphatically not to say that she was tried there. As Molinier has pointed out, the Inquisition economised its time by sitting at relatively few centres. The Cathedral at Toulouse was probably the nearest centre from the point of view of both time and place.

followed up an interview by writing.) In this letter she writes intelligently and rather scathingly of the pretty, pretty aspects of reincarnation. She said, 'I can only speak from personal experience when I say I remember evil people who existed in another life and I can only suppose that I'll remember them again one day. It would be pleasant to think they would all fade away in a puff of smoke, but I can't think so.'

She also wrote interestingly and critically on contemplation but I have no space to develop these themes. This is a pity because her views on life are inevitably moulded by her recollection of her past experience. It is worth while, however, to make one quotation from her letter because it expresses her experience of Catharism as revealed to her as a schoolgirl. It is interesting to put these against the views of the savants. I had apparently mentioned to her that one authority[4] had said that Cathar priests, who were known as Parfaits, were sometimes selected at birth. She wrote, 'I'm not prepared to accept that. Who wrote that and from where did he get his information? The Parfaits had above all to be spiritually pure, combining this with compassion and understanding. I think that he/she could only be a real sincere help and a source of comfort and consolation if he/she had experienced the struggles of life, desires of the flesh, sufferings and hardship. They reached their goal—their state of perfection —not by virtue of being born pure (no one is) but because they overcame human misery, ploughed through it, and discovered faith like a shaft of light in the darkness. If I ever felt the need for help I'd choose a person of this sort, i.e. spiritually pure but a *human* being rather than a celibate priest or nun or a person "born" pure and preserved artificially for a life of purity. If the writer of this book is an authority on the subject I can only say that in my opinion he isn't talking about pure Catharism but has been studying one of its offshoots—there were many.'

It will be noticed in speaking of the Parfaits that she allows for them being of both sexes. This means that she knew, in her early teens, from her dreams and visions, one of the most

[4] Schmidt, of the University of Strasbourg.

remarkable and distinguishing features of Catharism. Even in the thirteenth century women as well as men were admitted into the priesthood. After more than seven centuries the Anglican and Roman communities show little sign of catching up.

It is clear from what she recorded as a schoolgirl that she had understood, by direct experience, a great deal about the recruitment of the Parfaits. So many of these, both men and women, became Parfaits (fem. Parfaites) after having lived a married life and had children. The famous Esclarmonde of Foix had eight children before, with the agreement of her husband, she became a Parfaite. Here one must define one's terms a little. The Cathar aspirant prepared to become a Parfait by a life of chastity, meditation, fasting and good works. Special emphasis was laid on fasting. It was also necessary for him to abstain from animal food except fish. When they were judged fit to receive it by the elders of the Church they partook of the Consolamentum, the only sacrament recognised by the Cathars. The Consolamentum implied that from then on one lived only at the level of the Spirit and above the trammels of the flesh. The number of those who received the Consolamentum in the full vigour of life and who became Parfaits was naturally small. Many people received the Consolamentum on their deathbeds, revealing a natural desire to leave their abandonment of the flesh to the moment when it was in any case inevitable. It is important to remember this because Mrs. Smith's Roger died without being, as they said, 'consoled'.

In this letter Mrs. Smith expressed Dualist ideas of the forces of good and evil, 'two paths as it were, to choose'. She said the Cathars used to refer to children of light and children of darkness.

In a letter a week previously she had mentioned a quotation by some mediaeval scholar and asked me if I could help her locate it. I could not do so. Just previous to writing a further letter she had been to the library, picked up a book and was confronted immediately by a quotation. This kind of thing is a commonplace with people of this type.

74

19

On September 30th she wrote me again. She said that sometime after her second or third visit to me—in this letter she admitted she could not be specific as to dates—she started to dream in French. She found this surprising because the French in her dreams was fluent whereas such a description could not be applied to such French as she spoke by day on her holidays. She also said that Roger used to call her Puerilia. She comments, 'It isn't a French name—I looked it up long ago.' I later asked Professor Nelli about it but he did not think it was an Occitan word.[1] It has a Latin sound to it and may well have been a nickname. I suggested checking up on this in a Latin dictionary. I based this suggestion on the fact that Puella is Latin for girl. Mrs. Smith later consulted a vocabulary and found nothing.

She revealed how one of her requests for an interview was prompted by an inexplicable occurrence which made her feel decidedly uneasy. 'I telephoned a friend and arranged to meet her in Oxford. She had a Ford Anglia car and we planned to meet in a car park. She said as her car was a common make I should make a note of its registration and wait inside the car if she happened to be late leaving the office. It was pouring with rain on the day we were supposed to meet and I was soaked wandering around the car park looking for a Ford Anglia with the registration number I had written in my diary. My friend arrived rather late and asked why I hadn't waited in the car in the dry. I told her I couldn't find a car with the registration OFB 197 and she laughed and said I must have jotted down someone's 'phone number instead of her car number. I was quite prepared to believe her. I thought it was a queer thing to do but I didn't give it another thought.' Then she observed at a later date the number of my car which she had not previously noted and 'thought it

[1] The modern tendency is to group together the speech of the Languedoc and other allied languages under the heading of Occitan.

about time I was honest with you'. She could not have known previously the number of my car.

She spoke to someone whom she regarded as taking what she called 'a far too active interest' in extra-sensory perception. 'A bad thing, I think, because he calls it fun.' Nevertheless she arranged to listen in to him on the radio. It was only after she had heard the broadcast that she realised that the speaker, whom she had not met, was not billed to appear in the programme. She had seen the latter advertised in the paper but the names of the speakers did not include that of the person in question.

Another extract. 'I have discovered, and I'd be interested to know if you have too, that these gifts crash the time barrier, distance barrier and language barrier. For example, I had a line running through my mind, "Die Lorelei". I don't know it in English. I was thinking of it in German and I wasn't singing it aloud. My youngest daughter walked into the room and asked me out of the blue to sing her a song about a mermaid. She had not, as far as I know, heard this song before, she wouldn't in any case know what Die Lorelei was, and she knows not one word of German.'

The year previously she and her husband had flown to Beauvais. Before they went she had a dream of a plane upside down in an airfield. The flight to and from Beauvais was without incident but the following year, almost to the day on which they went to Beauvais, the identical plane in which they travelled and with the same pilot crashed on the airfield at Lympne. The plane landed upside down.

On another occasion she dreamt beforehand that a prominent Colonial Official had been killed. The next day she heard her precognition confirmed on a news flash. Her comment was, 'A few years ago this sort of thing could have terrified me but I don't worry about it any more. That man would have died whether I had remarked about it or not, wouldn't he? I used to think it was some kind of evil or black magic but it's not like that at all. I just keep slipping out of time as we know it, that's all. If we didn't talk about time as though it were a thing to be neatly classified as seconds, minutes or hours it would be different. It isn't like that, of course. Past, present and future are all part of an infinite time. Here and now is just an infinitesimal part of it.'

I consider I have quoted enough to illustrate this patient's psychicism. I wish I had more time to devote to her attitude towards life which naturally ties up with her Cathar past. But in the interests of precision I have to limit myself to the Cathar story.

20

From time to time I have wondered why the information given me by Mrs. Smith came out in such fragmentary fashion. Of course, as I have said previously, the most important delaying factor was her own frequent fear that she be thought mad or bad. Even after I had reassured her many times, it was surgically painful to her to part with the rather terrifying treasure of years. Were there other factors explaining the fact that her disclosures came in irregular spasms? One thing I am sure of and that is that she did not consistently sustain and force the process of recollection. She makes this clear in a slightly acid communication dated October 5th. I had previously written to her, in all good faith and with the best intentions, to the effect that under no circumstances, and certainly not to please me or at my instigation, should she *try* to recall things or force herself to concentrate. I can see now that I was maladroit but then I had never handled a case like this before and am not likely to do so again. Herewith her sharp reproof.

'Sometimes you make me cross. Is it really so difficult for you to understand me? I have been trying to cope with this business for twenty years. I have never been able to get rid of it and you'd be surprised at the measures I've taken. I have often been very much afraid and I've been made to suffer for it, but *never* have I taken advantage of it and don't ever intend to. I do *not* tire myself writing. I have *never* tried to force recollections.' (I did not suggest that she did this. I merely told her not to try too hard to remember by concentration.) 'Did you think these notes were the results of efforts like that? On the contrary, if ever I have forced myself to do anything it has been to try to forget, and the forcing did no good because I couldn't forget. You don't really know me at all well, do you? You certainly don't give me much credit for handling this sensibly. Strange though it may seem, I was trying to protect you. Your reluctance to be involved was obvious.' This is utterly and totally true. At one time I developed a quite feverish historical interest in the subject but I could never really accommodate myself to the idea that I had re-met somebody after seven hundred years. I see now how hard it was for the patient. I was more concerned with the fact that it made me feel uncomfortable.

The letter continues, 'I could have told you the whole thing en masse but I felt you were a little afraid and wanted to lead you gently. I frequently tried to drop hints to you and perhaps to tell you, but I was held back by a feeling that you weren't ready to take it.'

In another letter she told that she had given up the idea of going to Toulouse because she knew that she would never find anything by searching for it.

Another simple explanation for the episodic nature of her disclosures was simply the question of time. She was a busy housewife with a part-time job. The amount of time at her disposal was not sufficient to enable her to sort out and decipher promptly and completely a great deal of schoolgirl material written in great haste and stored away for years in a loft.

On the 21st October I received another letter. For the past five nights Mrs. Smith had had exactly the same dream and said, 'Quite frankly I am getting rather tired of it.' The setting is in France in the eighteenth century. I will not describe the dream in its entirety because we have to stick to the Cathars but the gist of it was that she was pursued by a mob, who possibly were after me, and that I behaved in a seemingly unheroic and

78

detached fashion. My excuse was something high-faluting to the effect that I had left the doors of the house open to the mob in order to prove that she had the freedom to escape from me if she chose, a rather masculine heads I win, tails you lose attitude. I describe the next bit of the dream because, though the latter is located principally in the eighteenth century, the end of it seems to go back very much earlier, as Mrs. Smith herself observes in a postcript to the letter written the day after. When the mob vanishes[1] her feet are cut and bleeding and I am washing them. As I do so she notices that I am wearing a thin gold chain which carries a pendant. The latter has a strange shape. She drew it out as follows ╫ . She goes on to say, 'There is a connection here, too, with the Middle Ages dream. In that one I wear a thin silver chain around my waist and the chain is fastened with something that looks exactly like the symbol I have tried to draw.'

This symbol occurred so vividly in my own night allusions that it is drawn out in my diary long before Mrs. Smith's letter of October 21st.

Mrs. Smith also draws attention to the fireplace. 'As in my dreams concerning the Middle Ages, the hearth in this dream, too, was in the centre of the room. This strikes me as absurd.' Here again, the dream which began in the eighteenth century is obviously harking back to the Middle Ages.

Later in the letter she said, 'I feel I've seen that symbol I've tried to draw. I thought for a minute it might be one of the Greek alphabet letters but it isn't.'

There is nothing further relevant to the Cathars in my diary till November 4th. At this time my wife and I were on holiday and on this day in particular we had dinner with Madame and Professor Nelli of Carcassonne. He told me that Fabrissa, as well as Alaïs, were common female names in the Languedoc of the

---

[1] Is this connected with my night illusion for years of a mob, with mediaeval faces, dancing and moving about rather wildly, in a sunlit square in a southern town?

Middle Ages. Alaïs was an abbreviated form of Azalaïs. (Another alternative form was Helis.) He said it might be profitable to study the records of the Inquisition to see if two such names appeared in any one case.

On the way back from France I called at the house of the friend in Paris who on a previous occasion had given me Zoë Oldenbourg's book. While I waited for him his wife gave me his father's journal. I saw first a remarkable poem about death composed by the old man. Then I turned over the pages to some date in the nineteenth century and found an entry to the effect that he, or at any rate somebody, was awaiting his next incarnation. When my friend returned I immediately burst out about reincarnation, said I believed in it and that it was referred to in his father's journal. He answered gravely and quietly that of course it was true but that one should never search backwards for one's incarnation or forwards to one's next. I had known my Parisian friend for twenty-seven years at the time of this interview. It is strange that over so many years I had learnt so little of his opinions or of how he was made. It seems I am able to lower a curtain which excludes enlightenment.

My diary points out that once again on this holiday I was more 'open' than I used to be. 'Mostly I am rendered replete by change of scene and the beauty of my surroundings. Or is it merely that I am different from what I used to be and functioning more frankly on another plane?'

21

In another letter from Mrs. Smith she was preoccupied with the question of deceiving me. She said she was very much mistaken about Mazerolles. Sometime ago she looked for it on the map. She could not find it and tried to forget about it. When I told her I had come across the place, she was not surprised until I described it. I told her that I saw a beautiful view, the village and little else. She commented, 'Mazerolles, as I see it, isn't like that at all. It wasn't a big town by any means but there was quite a community there.' She indicated that I must think her imagination was working overtime. She said she believed there was a castle here too. Now here again she is merely manifesting signs of sincerity. Mazerolles was a place of some importance in the Middle Ages. The Mazerolles family, I discovered later, were people of influence and encouraged and protected heretics. Professor Nelli, of Carcassonne, went to see the place after I gave him information from the patient and said that little remained of the thirteenth century, except the vestiges of the ramparts. I quote further from Mrs. Smith's letter. 'You said that Professor Nelli spoke of a Fabrissa and Alaïs who were together interrogated by the Inquisition. I did not know such records existed but as he has access to them would you please ask him if there is any indication that Fabrissa came from Mazerolles? I would like to know about Alaïs and if she came from a noble family, in which case there might be a slender hope of discovering if she had a brother named Roger. Are there any records in existence today giving records of the noble families in and around that area at the beginning of the thirteenth century?' This letter shows to what degree Mrs. Smith was ignorant of the very considerable knowledge of Cathar families which is still available from records of the Inquisition and elsewhere. Guiraud, in his *History of the Inquisition in the Middle Ages*, devotes a whole chapter to the heretical nobility of the Languedoc. This chapter contains numerous references to the central characters in this story.

On the 28th January, 1966, Mrs. Smith followed with a description of the hall in the castle at Mazerolles. She described a raised dais with several high backed chairs, a trestle-type table, rough benches, another table and a bench, and what she described again as the highly dangerous fireplace. She appended a drawing. I reproduce it herewith with her comments.

THE HALL AT MAZEROLLES, with Mrs. Smith's comments.

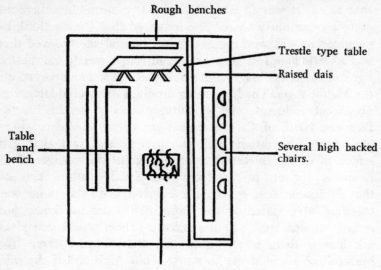

Rough benches

Trestle type table

Raised dais

Table and bench

Several high backed chairs.

Highly dangerous fireplace.

She also said that the owner of the castle must have been impoverished as they drank what appeared to be watered down wine. This could perfectly well accord with Cathar practice. She said there were not even glasses to drink from and that she drank 'from a metal cup shaped something like this'.

Drinking cup described by Mrs. Smith.

She was obviously unaware of the fact that drinking glasses were not in use in the Middle Ages.

She described herself as still bothered about the strange symbol referred to previously. She said that 'the silver girdle she wore was fastened by a buckle of that shape. It was even on our keys.'

Key worn by Puerilia (with Mrs. Smith's comments.)

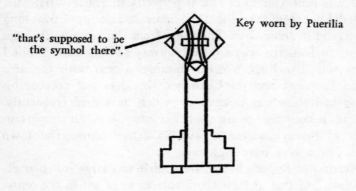

Key worn by Puerilia

"that's supposed to be the symbol there".

Ring worn by Roger

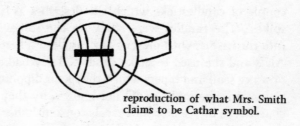

reproduction of what Mrs. Smith claims to be Cathar symbol.

She also included in her notes a drawing of the keys and a ring worn by Roger bearing the same symbol. She said that Roger wore the ring on his thumb. She indicated again that I should think her mad for making such statement. Again she was unaware that this was a mediaeval practice.

There is nothing distinctive about the drawing of the hall at Mazerolles. It could pass for any mediaeval hall. The drawings of the key and ring are more interesting. Perhaps those more learned than myself will find something of specific interest in them.

It will be seen later that she is obviously describing the home of Fabrissa de Mazerolles, who was a prominent Pairfaite and kept open house for heretics.

Speaking of Roger, she said she was pretty certain that his house was near Toulouse. This is perfectly in order. What Mrs. Smith did not seem to realise is the immense amount of travelling Cathars did in those days. The route from Carcassonne through Pamiers to Toulouse was a busy highway at that time. While I feel myself that Roger's main connection was with the area around Fanjeaux and the Corbières, this does not prevent his having had elsewhere possessions which he visited frequently. Guiraud makes the point that Fanjeaux was an important centre of heresy because it was an active commercial town situated on a very busy highway.

Referring to Roger's house, she said it was large but sparsely furnished, but that at least the fireplaces were not in the centre of the rooms. She remembered the bedroom in Roger's house. The bed was narrow with curtains around it, with a table with a couple of candlesticks which she describes as 'funny ones with spikes'. The candles were stuck on the spikes and not pushed into the base as with present day candles. When Roger was away Alaïs and she used to make candles. They had a large container of waxy stuff and tapers which they kept dipping in and allowing to harden. She said she did not know why they didn't go to the chandler to buy some. She reveals constantly her lack of historical acquaintance with the Middle Ages. There cannot have been chandlers at every street corner. She said that it was unfortunate but she could not remember Roger's surname. As we shall see in the next paragraph but one he had another name but she did not realise that this could be his surname. Nor could she remember her own name, because Roger always called her by what she described as, 'that stupid name which he must have invented'.

84

She said that he wore, 'the strangest night attire, a loose garment open at both sides. It had a row of tiny holes at the sides, laced with a fine cord rather like shoes are laced.'

On the 10th February I had a letter from her saying that she had been sorting out some shorthand notes which she had discovered some time previously in the loft. She said that a lot of it was completely undecipherable. She had forgotten she ever made this particular batch of notes. She said that in her younger days she used to write short stories and jotted down all sorts of ideas and that she probably put in her dreams for good measure. She said she could read the proper names because she was taught never to write them in shorthand. 'In one dream that I have forgotten I see that someone told me Roger had been taken to prison. But this man didn't give me a surname but mentioned the place Roger came from. He said Roger de Grisolles.' Again Mrs. Smith's account gains all the more in authenticity from her lack of historical knowledge. She does not realise that a very large proportion of names at that time merely included a Christian name, the word 'de' and the name of the place from which the person derived or in which one of his estates was situated. She said she was not quite sure whether it was Grisolles or Grifolles because from her writing she did not know whether she had used an s or an f. Grisolles is a small place about seventeen miles north of Toulouse.

This reference to Grisolles is interesting. On my previous summer holiday in France, before I had ever heard the name Grisolles, my wife and I were driving south to Toulouse. We had a picnic lunch. We did not wish to wait until we got beyond Toulouse so we stopped somewhere north of it. We drew up by a little canal. In going to, and leaving the site of, our picnic we did not notice the name of the adjoining village. Later, when Mrs. Smith and her family went down to the Pyrenees, she also did not want to stop in Toulouse because of her fear of it. She kept her fear to herself. They stopped and had lunch before they reached Toulouse. Again she did not realise until afterwards that she had stopped at Grisolles nor was she instrumental in arranging to stop. I myself only realised a year later that it was Grisolles at which my wife and I had stopped for our picnic. I discovered this by working it out later on the map. I confirmed that my observations were correct by another visit to the neighbourhood on a subsequent occasion.

Mrs. Smith was still puzzled about the distance between Mazerolles and Grisolles. She said there must be sixty miles between the two places and that 'It seems an awfully long way to go in those days with no transport but horses.' As I have said previously, this route was used constantly and the Cathars were accustomed to travelling long distances. Sixty miles would have appeared a mere nothing to the traveller in the Middle Ages, innured as he was to the long distances between towns and to going on pilgrimages.

She also pointed out with her extreme and almost fastidious honesty that she had spelt Mazerolles in her notes with one 'l' whereas it is now spelt with two. Alternative spellings for French names of places and persons were a commonplace in the Middle Ages, in addition to which spelling has changed considerably since those times.

In a letter of February 12th, 1968 she said, 'I believe that my life now is part of a pattern which has been repeated throughout the years. On the morning you came to this house many months ago I knew you would come.' She then repeated how my appearance in the snow recalled my coming through the storm seven centuries earlier. Then follows something of a heartcry which expresses her fear of having written so freely in the last few days of what she had kept secret for years. 'For God's sake don't show this letter to anyone. I know it isn't wise to write such things but I would have found it impossible to tell you in any other way. I should be grateful if you would please let me know if you are prepared to see me in a fortnight's time.'

In another letter round about this time she described the bed accommodation. 'Admittedly it had a curtained bed and must have given some privacy but other people shared that bedroom too.' Once again she reveals her unfamiliarity with mediaeval customs.

In this same letter she discussed the problems of good and evil and the creation of the world. 'I used to think that the world itself was alright and that the only evil around us was in man, but upon reflection I think the world was created with evil in it, when one considers that even in the very lowest forms of animal life some species will devour others to survive. Perhaps we are given the choice of which way to go, that is the choice of being guided towards spiritual purity or allowing ourselves to be corrupted. Is good perhaps only an issue when the question of choice is brought into the discussion?' This is all good Catharism. In addition, the latter question which she poses is concerned with the reconciliation of opposites. This is a primary feature of oriental philosophy, which, in its more transcendental aspects, requires that man should be beyond good and evil. Catharism, in relation to orthodox Christianity, is strongly tinged with oriental ideas. Non-resistance and a belief in re-incarnation are among the most striking resemblances which Catharism bears to the oriental religions.

Later in the letter she said, 'Sometimes through the wonder of the universe, nature, that is, in all its beauty, I find a new world is revealed to me and I understand vaguely the power and beauty of the Creator in an undefined presence which I call God. At moments like this I find peace, a peace which is experienced and cannot really be understood intellectually. I find myself thanking God. It isn't a question of my having a need to create a spiritual being but I have what I can only describe as a sense of unity. It is difficult to explain. Spiritual consciousness not only transcends the limitations of the bodily senses but transcends time and space too.' This extract reveals Mrs. Smith's capacity for the direct, mystical approach to God and reality. One should not need to add that in everyday life she is a practical and rather bustling type of person but one does so to reassure those for whom mysticism implies an incapacity for the ordinary affairs of life.

In a note about either a letter or an interview on February 1st, I have recorded her advice that I take care of myself particularly in cold, damp weather because Roger perished in a cold damp prison.

22

The date of the following extract is somewhere between the 13th and 17th February, 1966. This is a horrifically graphic description of the victim being burnt. One leaves it to the reader to judge whether the description adds to the authenticity of the experience.

Herewith is the extract. 'This is the dream about the burning. I thought at first that I would make a prècis of it but I decided it might be more interesting for you to read it exactly as I wrote it years ago. I have changed nothing but there are a few gaps where I found the shorthand impossible to transcribe.

'I don't think I have dreamt about dying before. I hope this dream is not a warning that I shall soon die. My brother says that if you tell anyone your dreams they won't come true. I can't tell anyone this, so if I write it that is almost the same thing, it won't come true. I wonder why I didn't scream. I couldn't have or someone would have told me about it and I would have woken up with a sore throat. I must have committed a fearful crime to deserve such an agonising death. So must the others. There were some more besides with me. They didn't seem afraid either. We all walked barefoot through the streets towards a square where they had prepared a pile of sticks all ready to set alight. There were several monks around singing hymns and praying. I didn't feel grateful. I thought they had a cheek to pray for me. I must be rather a wicked person. I don't think wicked things when I am awake, but I dream awful things. I hated those monks being there to see me die. A girl at school once said she dreamt of Christ's crucifixion. I would rather be crucified than burnt.

88

'The pain was maddening. You should pray to God when you're dying, if you can pray when you're in agony. In my dream I didn't pray to God. I thought of Roger and how dearly I loved him. The pain of those wicked flames was not half so bad as the pain I felt when I knew he was dead. I felt suddenly glad to be dying. I didn't know when you were burnt to death you'd bleed. I thought the blood would all dry up in the terrible heat. But I was bleeding heavily. The blood was dripping and hissing in the flames. I wished I had enough blood to put the flames out. The worst part was my eyes. I hate the thought of going blind.[1] It's bad enough when I'm awake but in dreams you can't shake the thoughts away. They remain. In this dream I was going blind. I tried to close my eyelids but I couldn't. They must have been burnt off, and now those flames were going to pluck my eyes out with their evil fingers. I didn't want to go blind.

'The flames weren't so cruel after all. They began to feel cold. Icy cold. It occurred to me that I wasn't burning to death but freezing to death. I was numb with the cold and suddenly I started to laugh. I had fooled those people who thought they could burn me. I am a witch. I had magicked the fire and turned it into ice.'

On the 17th February, 1966 I received another letter from Mrs. Smith, in which she said, 'The dreams have all been rather scrappy and I never dreamt the events in the order that they happened, but I did at least write it in some sort of order. I should guess it was all written up about 1949 to 1950 but the notes aren't dated. In 1954[2] I started writing the novel.' She then said that she was enclosing some extracts which she had collected from her previous writings. She added, 'Perhaps now you will understand why I behaved so badly when I first met you.' She was referring to the fact that she did not tell me straightaway

[1] It is interesting that at times I, too, have had this dread of being blind to the degree that at night, after the lights have been switched off, I have switched them on again in order to convince myself that I could still see.
[2] The date of her first visit to France, with her experience of the déjà vu phenomenon, and of the beginning of my Menières syndrome.

that the dreams stopped after the first interview. 'It was a hell of a shock to walk into that room and see you there, and I thought my mental condition was worse than I feared.'

On the 17th February she sent me a long extract of what she could fathom from the shorthand notes. What follows is exactly as she wrote it at the time. 'I could write a book about Roger and it would not take any effort at all. I have dreamt all of it at some time or other and it is all very easy to set down on paper. It would never be published. I couldn't bear that. It is a comfort to know that other girls dream of lovers. I wish I didn't have the uneasy feeling that this is different. I don't want to live in a world of fantasy and that world is so real to me, but if I write it maybe I shall get it out of my system. I will never get married. Tom[3] won't like that. I must have a natural aversion to marriage. I am not even married to Roger in my dream.'

The natural aversion to marriage could tie up with certain Cathar ideas held by the Parfaits. In the past it has been generally held by the historians that the Cathar priesthood regarded marriage as sinful. One should emphasise that this is an exaggerated and distorted conception of Cathar doctrine.

'I fell in love with him that very night he came to our house in the snowstorm. I tried not to stare at him but I was terribly aware of his nearness. I couldn't have moved further away from him if I had wanted to. The place was too small. I have just called it a house but it was little more than a hovel. One room, that's all, and he seemed to occupy every inch of it. I am sure there was no upstairs. The only furniture was a rough bench and a table. It was almost as dark inside as it was out, for the small window had no glass in it and the opening was covered with a crude wooden shutter to keep out the elements.' (Again Mrs. Smith is revealing her ignorance of the Middle Ages. Glass in the thirteenth century was only the perquisite of the very rich and of special institutions like the Church.) 'I was filled with joy because the weather was bad and it was necessary for him to stay the night. That night I kissed him when he was asleep. We

[3] A boy friend.

were all sleeping with our clothes on, on the floor around the fire and in the dim light I could see his hand. He wore a ring on his thumb. I moved nearer to him, very slowly, for I didn't want any of them to wake up. When I was close enough I kissed his hand and felt happy. I had never kissed a man before.

'Roger used to go to meetings at Montbrun and I went to the meetings too. I only went to see him. I knew my father would be angry about the meetings and about Roger and we had to be careful. There were plenty of places where we could be alone. The countryside was wooded. Roger used to talk a lot at the meetings but when he was with me we would often walk miles holding hands and scarcely saying a word.'

Mrs. Smith mentions Montbrun. There are two such places (one is spelt Monbrun) near Toulouse. One is, as the crow flies, 32 kilometres to the north-west of the city, the other is 16 kilometres to the south. There is another Montbrun 32 kilometres north-west of Foix and another a little north of the Corbières in the Aude. All these Montbruns were in regions staunchly devoted to Catharism. Mrs. Smith persists that the Montbrun in which she remembers Roger preaching was in the neighbourhood of Montgaillard near Foix and that it has either disappeared or its name has been changed in the course of the centuries.

In contemplating her association with Roger one must realise that relationships between people of different social status were freer in the Languedoc and in the Midi in general than elsewhere in Europe.

'He looked a bit like a monk when he was dressed. He always wore a loose garment almost down to his ankles, with a girdle around his waist.[4] His cloak was long, too, and he had a hood attached to it. He really did look very much like a monk if it hadn't been for the colour of his clothes. I think he liked blue because nearly everything he wore was that colour.'

She is obviously describing the garb of a Cathar priest. What

[4] She means a girdle over his outer garment. If it had been a thin cord worn next to his skin this would have been of greater interest. It is often said, probably erroneously, that Cathar priests wore such a cord beneath their clothing.

she says about the colour of his clothes being dark blue is of immense importance. All the historians until the last three or four years have said that the Cathar priests invariably wore black. That this was not inevitably so has only been proved in the last few years by Monsieur Duvernoy. His book was published in 1965. Mrs. Smith's observations were made, as near as I can estimate, twenty-six years ago. Because of this remarkable and important fragment of far memory, in insisting on which she can be said to have stood alone, it is necessary to take seriously her other insistent preoccupations as, for example, her statement that the girdles of Parfaits were buckled and not tied and that Catharism was not the austere and gloomy religion described by its detractors. Certainly so far as her statements about buckles and the signs designed on them are concerned, one must wait for the evidence, bearing always in mind Professor Nelli's contention that when in doubt one should go by the patient.

The Cathar Parfait had to observe complete sexual abstinence. It will be asked what a Cathar priest was doing consorting with a girl. This, too, must wait for further explanation. In the meantime it seems obvious that Roger was not a fully-fledged priest.

'The day my father beat me and sent me away from home was one of the happiest days of my life. I went to Roger with nothing but the clothes I wore, and I didn't even have any shoes. I think I had some. I can't remember not having them when I went walking with Roger. I must have left them behind. His house was on top of a hill and the road leading to it was rough and stony. He lived in a large place, not a castle, but something like a fortified house. We passed through a gate in a high wall and then into a yard which we crossed and into the main door. I felt reluctant to go into his house dressed as I was. I wished I had had something prettier to wear. Inside the main door were a few more steps which went up into a large hall. It was ever so big, and there were several benches, chairs and tables. There were several other people in the house. They were all very kind to me and I sat by the fire at the far end of the hall. They were cooking something. I don't know what it was. During the evening I sat and watched him whilst he played a game with another man. A game with something like a draught board, with rather elaborately carved counters and dice.

'He took me to his room and showed me where we would sleep. The bed was high and around it were blue curtains made of woollen material. For me it was luxurious because I had never slept in a bed before. Roger undressed and put on a loose garment. I thought it strange that he should wear special clothes for bed. In the morning I discovered his ring had bruised my shoulder.

'We were sublimely happy. Times were difficult and Roger was often away. I used to spend my time with a sweet kind woman who lived with us.' (This was almost certainly Alaïs[5] (Helis) but could have been Fabrissa.) 'She was older than I was. She was a great source of comfort. I was like a lost soul without Roger but she understood how much I loved him and how I worried about him. He caught cold so easily and would often return home soaked to the skin and worn out through lack of sleep. He was terribly ill once and I thought he was going to die. I wouldn't leave him and I slept by his side trying to warm him with my body. He had a high fever but was shivering. The bedroom had no fire.[6] There were two candlesticks on the table in the room and they contained candles which were kept lit all the time. I don't know why no one called a doctor. Thank God he got better because if he died I should have had nothing to live for. He used to make up his own medicines from plants and things he obtained in the woods and fields. He was so precious to me. I was pregnant at the time and Roger was scarcely on his feet again before the baby was due. It was a girl but she only lived a short while. I was terribly unhappy about it and Roger said we would have another. I thank God I didn't know then it wasn't to be. There was so much sickness, suffering, killing and fear. Life became harder. We were uncertain and situations changed rapidly from

[5] Alaïs was Roger's sister and presumably more likely to be concerned with him, provided she accepted, as she seems to have done, his liaison with a peasant girl.
[6] What did she expect in the thirteenth century?

day to day. Our love seemed to be the only safe and sure thing in the world.'

One's comment on the above paragraph is again that Mrs. Smith is assuming that doctors were as available in those days as now. What she did not know was that the Cathars were especially addicted to medicine, in fact it was one of the accusations made against them by the Catholics that they used their position as doctors to propagandise in favour of the heresy. Perhaps Roger, with his herbal remedies, also had medical interests.

Here I have to admit that I had no confidence in one of Mrs. Smith's statements. This was when she described how when Roger was ill they gave him loaf sugar. For better or worse I could not believe that this product existed in the thirteenth century. Professor Nelli makes it clear that Mrs. Smith was right and I was wrong. In his latest book *La Vie Quotidienne des Cathares*, published in the summer of 1969, Professor Nelli describes the antics of the somewhat unorthodox curé of Montaillou. This gentleman, after his final visit to his mistress, sent her, a short time afterwards, some loaf sugar described by Professor Nelli as a food stuff very rare at this epoch.

Towards the end of August, 1969 I wrote to tell her what I had read on the subject of loaf sugar in Professor Nelli's latest book. She wrote as follows on the 31st. 'I would have replied to your letter on Friday but at the back of my mind I was sure there was some detail concerning sugar which I had overlooked. I woke up last night and remembered what it was, though it doesn't seem very important. The sugar was kept *locked*. I don't think this could have been because of its high cost. The family were wealthy and they weren't misers. Probably because sugar was very scarce and extremely difficult to come by.

'I see in your letter you mention how Roger was fed on *lump* sugar. I wrote, or should have written, *loaf* sugar.' (She did. I wrote lump sugar because I honestly thought it was the same as loaf sugar and because the former description was my method of translating *pain de sucre*.) Mrs. Smith continued, 'Lump sugar conjures up a picture of neat little cubes such as one sees today, but what Roger had wasn't like that at all. They were more uneven pieces broken from one large lump. He only had it when he was ill'.

In the history of sugar in a Tate and Lyle booklet there is a passage which says, 'Throughout the years sugar was used as a medicine for practically every ailment under the sun. Arab doctors recommended it for diseases of the chest'. The influence of Arab medicine was great in the Languedoc of the thirteenth century. As we shall see later Roger not only died of a chest infection but was subject to such a condition for some time before his death.

Her long statement of February 17th, 1966 continues as follows. 'The woman in the house used to say that Roger and I should be married. She kept repeating it was not safe for me to be unmarried but I don't know why. I didn't mind. We weren't really a wicked pair, though. We both loved God, we said prayers and went to religious meetings. They weren't like proper Church meetings. Neither of us went to Church. There was a church nearby which was a bit strange inside. There were seats in the chancel presumably for priests but no seats at all in the nave. No wonder we didn't go there. I wouldn't have wanted to stand up all the time.' One need hardly repeat that this reveals again her ignorance of mediaeval customs.

'I hope I never dream again of that heartbreaking moment when that man came riding up and told me Roger had been taken to a prison. I wanted to go there to him but the man stopped me and said I should be mad to show myself and that I must leave Roger's house straightaway before they came for me. I didn't seem to care much about being caught if only I could have been with Roger, but the man said that the prisoners were allowed to have wives but not concubines. It must have been a peculiar prison if they allowed men to have their wives with them. I was filled with worry about Roger. I could not bear the thought of leaving his house in case he should return and find me gone. But he had told me I was to go immediately to

Fabrissa if anything happened to him, so that night I left with his sister. Roger had been very careful to tell me I must take some money with me. It was in a thick coarsely woven bag rather like a miniature sack off-white in colour. It was plated round the base and the top and there was a cord which pulled it tightly together at the top. It was heavy. There was no paper money in it but lots of coins.' (Mrs. Smith knew much of Cathar life in the thirteenth century but not that paper money was not in use at that time.)

This is pretty conclusive. She was going with Helis (Alaïs) to Fabrissa.[7] The latter was a person of influence, sister-in-law to Helis and, according to the records of the Inquisition, a notorious protector of heretics. The fact that Mrs. Smith says so clearly on this, as on other occasions, that Alaïs was Roger's sister, indicates clearly that the Roger with whom we are dealing was Roger Isarn, son of Bec de Fanjeaux and Aude de Tonnens. I will discuss Roger's identity more fully in the later chapters.

'We stopped en route at somebody's house. I don't remember the house but it was there I heard the news of Roger's death. I wished to forget that house that day and everything connected with it. The woman who told me was very kind and sympathetic but I knew before she told me what she was going to say. I didn't want her to voice the words but I was so filled with horror that I couldn't stop her. She said he had died in prison of a chest infection. I hate to think of what those terrible people must have done to him. I wanted to die. Life from that moment on was a cold, meaningless existence. Without love there is no such thing as life, no hope, nor joy. I told his sister I would go away alone to die quietly. I was going to commit suicide. Not as people generally commit suicide. It was an easy way out of life. I didn't want to live. I would give up eating until I became so weak I would die. His sister wouldn't let me do it. She said that what I had loved most about him was life. He had given me life and I would be wrong to throw away the precious gift he had offered

[7] The reader may remember that our first clue was Roger's statement, 'If anything happens to me go to Fabrissa.'

me. Not a very convincing argument and I don't think I would be convinced now by such words but in my grief I was past being able to think for myself. I allowed her to persuade me to live on without him but I never really succeeded. Nothing was ever the same again. It never will be.

'It would be wonderful if it were possible to find a man I could love like I loved him. I know I have thought I have been in love several times and I think I am in love now. Possibly Tom and I would be happy if we married. Deep in my heart I am still full of love for that man in my dreams. I feel I belong to him and no one else. I like Tom kissing me. Sometimes I think it would be wonderful to be married but not a fraction as wonderful as it was with Roger who was never my husband but the most precious lover I have known or will ever know.'

I must admit that I found it hard to accept Mrs. Smith's statement that in the prison in which Roger was incarcerated the men were allowed to have their wives visit them. By this time I felt her story to be completely valid but I was prepared for her to slip up sometimes over the details. I could not credit that the Inquisition would permit its imprisoned victims to be visited by their wives. Once again I was wrong and Mrs. Smith right. On August 25th, 1969 my doubts were put at rest by Professor Nelli's *La Vie Quotidienne des Cathares*. He points out that people could be imprisoned, by order of the Inquisitors, between two interrogations. The technical term was *emmuré*, the Mur being the prison of the Inquisition. The people thus immured were treated differently from those definitely sentenced to imprisonment for life or of long duration. In the Inquisitorial prisons at Pamiers and Carcassonne the unconvicted suspects were allowed to encounter and talk with other detainees of their own sex.

Professor Nelli tells us that at Carcassonne temporary prisoners were allowed to receive the visits of their wives. This bears out completely Mrs. Smith's statement.

Roger was apprehended at St. Papoul. Carcassonne was surely the nearest Inquisitorial prison. Measured as the crow flies, the distances from St. Papoul to Pamiers and Carcassonne respectively are not much different. But St. Papoul is quite near the main road from Carcassonne to Toulouse and we know that even in the thirteenth century this was a very busy highway. In those days the route from St. Papoul to Pamiers must have been very crosscountry. It seems pretty clear that Roger died in the prison at Carcassonne.

23

In a letter of February 20th, 1966 she found some further old notes when sorting out her papers before going into hospital. These notes were concerned with dress. Puerilia's father used to wear a short knee-length tunic. Roger wore his clothes at ankle length. 'In Roger's house there were lots of people and some of them wore outfits similar to my father's and some like Roger. Surely there couldn't have been two different styles of clothes for men. It doesn't make sense, does it?' She is not allowing for the fact that people of different social standards wore different clothes in the Middle Ages and also for the fact that Roger was some kind of priest. She said, 'Everyone in the house prayed night and morning but it hadn't occurred to me that he might have been a Cathar preacher. He was very earthy if he was'.

I saw Mrs. Smith on February 25th. She told me that Roger wore a girdle with a purse containing a book. This is of fundamental importance. Cathar priests always carried round with them the Gospel according to St. John. She also mentioned a knife he used for eating and for cutting things up outside in the woods. She pointed out that he wore his hair long. This is again in accordance with facts. Cathar priests wore their hair long and it was never tonsured.[1] On this day she told me that her revelations could be sparked off by trivial incidents. Her daughter

[1] This question of tonsure or no was sometimes a matter of life or death. Some of the more brusque among the harassed Languedocien knights were inclined, following the Catholic persecution, to take revenge on people wearing clerical garb. Examination of the scalp to see if there was a tonsure or evidence of its previous existence could be crucial for the cleric.

washed her hands and then her mother washed hers in the same water. This set her off remembering that Roger used to wash first and then the other people used the same water afterwards. I am not sure if this was any kind of Cathar rite. She made a further comment about Grisolles, saying that 'the house there was on a hill but there was also some kind of chapel in the valley'.

She referred again on this occasion to the illness she had the first time she went to France in August, 1954, and which coincided with the beginning of my Meniére's syndrome. It is interesting to recall that my interest in mysticism dates very postively from this time. I remember especially reading Dean Inge's Mysticism whilst convalescing. My interest in Buddhism also intensified. This is important because of the likenesses between Buddhism, with its belief in non-resistance, reincarnation, abstention from flesh foods, etc. with Catharism. Also it was at this time that I had two experiences of being beyond time and beyond good and evil. The beginning of Mrs. Smith's extrasensory career was ushered in by headache and two attacks of unconsciousness. It is reasonable to suppose that my Meniéres, another illness which can be one of the 'out of time' variety, was an essential accompaniment of the initiation of my extra-sensory experiences.

In a letter written to me on February 25th she said she had not read much about Cathar doctrine. She said that she had to be careful about reading about Catharism in order not to confuse 'what I have read with what I know. I wish very much that I could remember some of the things Roger spoke about at those meetings. I know he thought the Virgin Birth was a lot of nonsense and often said that Roman Catholics were a superstitious lot. Yet in the few books on Catharism I have read the authors seem to go all out for accusing the Cathars of being superstitious. I don't believe they were.' She is perfectly right here. The authors of such books do not seem able to distinguish between sheer superstition and genuine psychic gifts. It is almost certain that the latter were considerably developed in the Cathar priesthood. Such gifts would tend to be manifested because of their mystical approach and the ascetic nature of their lives. The fact that the Inquisitors so often accused them of superstition and occultism is only to be expected. This would be the natural Inquisitional translation of gifts of healing, clairvoyance etc. just as, for example, Cathar chastity was, from the point of view of biased Catholicism, almost inevitably regarded as either hypocrisy or a cloak for perversion.

She continued, 'Theirs was a religion of freedom and joy and not pervaded by fanatical and morbid asceticism as some people would have us believe.' Here again I feel she is absolutely right. The critics of Catharism fail to distinguish between the Parfait and the ordinary *croyant*. The latter were not required to fast and mortify the flesh any more than the average Hindu or Roman Catholic, even though both Hindu and Catholic priests may regularly practise asceticism as well as meditation and other such disciplines.

She said that it is a great pity that, 'the great organised religious bodies fail to recognise the simplicity of Christ. His true philosophy of life has been lost to them and how can it be otherwise when He has been imprisoned in the Church? I am not trying to belittle the good of the Church, which is a necessary place of comfort for some, but an enlightened preacher once wrote that the great use of the Church is to enable people to do without it.

'Peace for me isn't the hallowed feeling one sometimes feels in Church. It comes to me in a mind divorced from enslaving matter and all material things. You know me well enough to know I don't live in a blissful spiritual state all the time but my idea of heaven is peace.' She then makes a very significant remark. 'I don't think there is any mystery about evil—is it not just simply the absence of good?' This is getting on to the being beyond good and evil which is a feature of oriental philosophy. Catharism was influenced by transcendental philosophy of such origin. A philosophic connection between Catharism and Buddhism is revealed in the celebrated story of Barlaam and Josophat.

Referring back to the occasion when she nearly died of peritonitis and when she screamed when the priests appeared with the Last Sacrament, she said that her father told her that she 'kept babbling on about having another baby and I was only about thirteen or fourteen at the time.' This refers back to her having lost her child in the thirteenth century.

It is interesting that her father should have spoken to her in such a manner. This, after all, happened twenty-six years ago when she was only thirteen and before topics of discussion had reached their present degree of liberty or licence. It seems possible that her father was similarly constituted to herself. The fact that, as we shall see later, he kept her scraps of mediaeval French poetry, is also significant in this connection.

Referring to clothing, she said she could not remember wearing the tall pointed hairdress one often sees in pictures of mediaeval people. 'The older women wore wimples which looked a bit nun-like, but the younger women wore their hair in a kind of net arrangement but most of the time I didn't even have that. I kept my hair loose with just a metal band on the top of the head. I am inclined to think it was more ornamental than useful. The mediaeval costumes I see occasionally are to my mind far too dressy and fancy. The clothes I remember are a lot plainer than that.

'I have never seen in any pictures the type of shoes Roger wore. They were leather and had a strap which buttoned round the ankles. Most peculiar things but I am quite certain that's what they were like.' This reference to shoes is interesting. Both the Cathar and the Vaudois priests wore peculiar shoes and one of the names attributed to them derived from this practice.

She talked also about a peculiar comb with two lots of teeth which Roger used for his hair which, as well as being long, was worn in a fringe.

She again referred to other dreams occurring in France but not in the Middle Ages. This is interesting because, whilst I have no personal recollection of the thirteenth century, I have some evidence of two other incarnations, in both of which I feel I have been in France and in one of which I am sure I was a sailor. I do not, however, labour this particular point because my only evidence is one vision and a certain amount of intuition.

She told me in a letter dated February 28th, 1966 that her mother was psychic and had a knack of being right with her predictions. This prejudiced Mrs. Smith against psychic matters because her mother tended to be proud of her accomplishments.

On the 2nd March she wrote a very good and long letter from which I shall quote extracts. I had expressed regret that I could not have more direct information about the Cathar faith. Her response was as follows. 'Yes, the Cathar faith was simple, but deceptively simple and much too honest for a great many people to accept. To embrace such a faith needed courage—courage to see oneself and life as it is. So many were afraid to do this and fear is the breeding ground of hate. That is why they were persecuted—out of pure fear by people who could not and would not see life as it is, a fractional moment of time and just a stage in the ultimate fulfilment of perfection. This truth came to me not when I was trying to evade suffering but when I could not stand the weight of my own burdens and also find surplus strength to help others with theirs. I know that we truly cannot lay up for ourselves treasure on earth. To become part of a universal mind it is necessary to take these things gently. A flower bud doesn't strain and struggle to unfold itself, it does it naturally and the wind and rain do not harm it. That's simple enough, isn't it, but look around at the mad rush and scramble of people trying to live and see how difficult it is for them to accept this truth. The Cathar faith naturally attracted its share of cranks and fanatics and the "offshoots" give it a bad name. True Catharism was never anything but faith pure and simple.'

In letters written early in March she returns to the question of the symbol on the ring and buckle. For some reason or other she identified it with one of the signs of the Zodiac.[2] She said

[2] The Cathars were definitely interested in astrology. This was used as a charge against them. The accusation came under the heading of witchcraft. Yet the Catholic monarchy of that day and afterwards employed Court astrologers.

that she felt it was the sign of Pisces. She said she had been seeing this sign for years. On the 18th March she received a letter from a world-famous professor of Mediaeval History to whom she had written previously. In her first letter she had raised the question with him of this sign which was on the buckle of Roger's girdle. She had asked him if it was a Cathar symbol and he had replied in the negative. Very charmingly he then wrote again, spontaneously, saying that, when going through some mediaeval manuscripts, he had discovered a symbol in the margin which resembled the one she had drawn out for him and this symbol was said to be Cathar.

On the 18th March I had a letter from her to the effect that, 'If you are prepared to take my word for it, the distinctive girdles worn by Parfaits were definitely buckled and not tied. I remember possessing one myself but I can't think why.' Later I wrote to Monsieur Duvernoy and asked if he could enlighten me on this point. He said there was no certain information as to the girdles worn by Parfaits.

Mrs. Smith thought that possibly she was some kind of preacher but rejected positively the idea that she was ever a Parfaite. The latter possibility is out of the question. On the other hand, she could well have done some preaching. The Cathars were great believers in the spoken word and there is some evidence that they were assiduous propagandists.

24

On the 30th March she returned to the Ashridge theme. She said this place had kept cropping up everywhere she went and that for some strange reason people kept talking about the place to her. She seemed to have covered the same grounds in her investigations as I did but not so thoroughly. She thought there was some connection between the Bonshommes at Ashridge and the Society of Gaunt. On April 1st she seemed satisfied that the Bonshommes at Ashridge were not Cathars. She said that she had been interested in how they wore their hair. She had received a letter that morning saying that the Bonshommes of Ashridge had tonsures according to the statutes of the College. This latter is further evidence against their being openly practising Cathars.

On April 5th I saw her by appointment. For some reason or other, during this interview, we started to talk about trees. I should say that for several years I literally suffered agony at seeing trees cut down. Mrs. Smith was afflicted in the same way and was instrumental in saving an avenue of trees which was threatened in her locality. It appears that in the thirteenth century Roger was in the habit of walking a great deal in the woods. I have always felt that my own feeling about trees was not merely aesthetic. I have felt that there was something specially sacred about them and that they offered protection. It may well be that in the past I needed their cover and that my agonies when they were cut down was a recollection of a former experience. It was interesting that if a tree was blown down in a gale I did not register the same anguish.

Mrs. Smith, or perhaps it is better to refer to her thirteenth-century incarnation as Puerila, wore grey before Roger's death and black afterwards. The dress was always very dowdy. When she went to the stake she was dressed in white.

It was suggested to Mrs. Smith by an acquaintance that a study of watermarks might provide a clue to the nature of the symbol occurring on Roger's buckle and the key she had carried. She wrote to a firm of paper makers in Hertfordshire on the subject of water marks. In the Middle Ages and afterwards paper making was an industry inevitably associated with heresy. This applied particularly in the case of the Albigensians. The latter used water marks in order to further propaganda for their religion. Hertfordshire is one of the countries in England where paper making is most active. There are paper mills at Watford and King's Langley. Ashridge which, in spite of the evidence, I still hold to have had Cathar affiliations, is situated in Hertford-shire. Mrs. Smith confirmed for me on this day that her grand-mother's birthplace was certainly the Ashridge in Hertfordshire.

There is a fascinating sequel to this story. On January 25th the following year she reverted again to the theme of water-marks and the reputation of the Albigensians as great paper-makers. She suggested that I write to Sir A. B., a member of a distinguished family of heretical ancestors and engaged in paper-making. On the same day I was told by another friend, living over sixty miles away and unknown to Mrs. Smith, that she had just met Sir A. B. for the first time that day. This friend, whom I will refer to as C for the sake of convenience, described Sir A. B. as 'having history written in his face and as having the dentition of the Middle Ages'. Both C's parents were dentists.

Four days previously C handed me a book on French cathedrals. The book was open at a page which contained a quotation from one of Madame X's efforts. I was greatly surprised because I did not think the latter were known except to a few people.

The chain of communication involving C continued. Not more than a week later a colleague asked if she could bring along to meet me a Frenchman from Narbonne who was staying with her father. She knew my interest in the Cathars and it appeared that Monsieur N, her father's guest, had a friend who lived in the neighbourhood of Foix and who was regarded as a great authority on the subject. Unfortunately I could not see him on the day she suggested nor was it possible to arrange another date. During the next week C had booked to go to France but the crossing was cancelled because of rough weather. At Southampton she saw and took pity on a Frenchman who seemed very much at a loose end because of the cancellation. She took him back to her home town and showed him the sights until the next sailing. The man she rescued was, of course, the guest of my doctor's friend's father. The latter lived eighty miles distant from my charitable friend. This is another of those synchronisations of events which are constantly occurring in this story and of which I have only quoted a limited number. These synchronisations and the Cathar revelations arise on the same plane of psychic activity.

This particular day was noteworthy because I read in Guiraud's *History of the Inquisition* that Fabrissa de Mazerolles was a Parfaite. She was described as a relative of Blanche de Laurac and as living at Gaja. I learnt also from Guiraud that Cathar reunions were held at Mazerolles, Gaja, Laurac and Fanjeaux. I will not go deeply now into what I found in Guiraud at this time because I was very busy at this period and my reading was rapid and spasmodic.

25

In a letter of April 5th Mrs. Smith said she had been reading Zoë Oldenbourg's *Massacre at Montségur*. She encountered for the first time a description of the murder of the Inquisitors at Avignonet. She honestly but very naïvely says that the incident did not strike a chord in her memory. For a start she could not be expected to remember everything. Secondly she was not present at the massacre. She wonders ingenuously if the Pierre de Mazerolles mentioned by Zoë Oldenbourg and her own nocturnal visitor were the same man. Beyond any doubt they were. The family connections of de Mazerolles and his complicity in the murder are established beyond any doubt and will be dealt with later.

She did, however, recall enough to say, 'Those men' (i.e. the murderers at Avignonet) 'were not true Cathars. They fought for personal power and financial gain.' There is more to it than that because they were also concerned in destroying the records of the Inquisition in order to preserve the security of people compromised because of their Cathar loyalties. The situation was comparable to the destruction by Resistance Movements in the last war of Gestapo records. But she was uncannily right about the financial gain, certainly as it appeared to Pierre de

Mazerolles. This comes out clearly in the deposition of Imbert de Salas which I will quote later.

Speaking from her own personal recollections, she said that over the years the doctrines and philosophy of Catharism have been distorted so as to be unrecognisable. This is true enough. The Inquisition's propaganda success, the effect of which has lasted seven hundred years, is as impressive as the completeness with which they exterminated the Cathars. She continued, 'The Endura is a perfect example,' i.e. of the distortion of truth by propaganda. It may be remembered that the Endura was described as committing suicide by fasting.

She continued. 'They'—she is referring to the Parfaits—'freely associated with believers who quite frequently led lives of immorality.' She is here dealing with a question constantly raised by Catholic antagonists of Catharism. Guiraud, a not unreasonable historian, almost moans over this particular point. The argument runs that if the Parfaits led lives of complete asceticism why did they associate with, and receive hospitality from, people living unmarried with their mistresses etc? This argument applied logically would mean that any Catholic priest having any social relations whatever with a person leading an immoral life would be guilty of the worst hypocrisy. This argument is ludicrous but it has been advanced seriously by a number of those Catholic writers whose minds and heads cease to work when their attention is focused on what they call heresy which, for practical purposes, means sometimes the rest of the world.[1] There is a particular point of interest illuminated by Mrs. Smith's thirteenth-century experience. When she says, 'They freely associated with believers who quite frequently led lives of immorality', she is, in using the term 'freely associated', expressing something which has troubled a little the most steadfast defenders of Catharism. It is noteworthy, for example, that many of the garrison of Montségur had with them what were described

[1] One realises that Catholics as a whole are more open minded these days but the liberation of the Catholic Church is of recent origin and we do not know yet if its gains will be consolidated.

as their mistresses. She herself goes on to explain the matter. 'Such people, i.e. those who led lives of immorality, were accepted by the Parfait but of course they were, for a doctor seeks to heal the sick, not the healthy.' This may not suit the prejudice of certain critics, but it is in line with Christian practice as exemplified by Christ.

In this letter Mrs. Smith showed a reversal of front with regard to Catharism and her own potentialities. She said that I need not hesitate to ask her questions or to tell anyone else about her or her experiences. She said, 'Always bear in mind though that most of the details I know are just memories and some-times not the slightest bit in accordance with books on Cathars, for which the authors have presumably made strict, painstaking research.' Here she is flattering the diligence of authors. Though I cannot claim to be an authority on the subject, I myself have been horrified at the way in which reputable historians have accepted as evidence isolated statements by one peasant extracted under interrogation and torture. Anyone with any working knowledge of Catharism can trace statements, repeated time and time again in standard works to one contemporary and biased source. It must be remembered that we are indebted for the most part to the Inquisition for contemporary accounts of Catharism.

On the evening of the day on which I received this letter I had a telephone call from her. She had just been deciphering some further notes she had discovered. As far as she could make out these were made in her later teens, round about the age of seventeen or eighteen. She discovered the names Sicard, Guiraud and de Levis. She did not know how they were connected with each other. The connection is clear. Sicard, Guiraud and a brother Gaucerand, not mentioned by Mrs. Smith, were members of the entourage of de Levis. The latter had displaced the old Cathar Seigneurs from the estate of Mirepoix in the years preceding the fall of Montségur. Nevertheless we shall see that the brothers remained at heart stout Cathars. She also found a reference to Bishop Imbert. He preached to an assembly at Mazerolles. She went there accompanied by Fabrissa.

Mrs. Smith discovered a warning to keep away from St. Papoul. It transpired later that this was the place where Roger was apprehended. She was warned by somebody called Savaric to keep away from this place.

On April 15th she wrote again, 'I must go in the loft sometime to see if I have any names jotted down in old school rough notebooks. I often noted a name which came into my head, especially if it was unusual.'

Referring to her discovery in Guiraud that Fabrissa de Mazerolles was a prominent protector of heretics, she commented, 'There were quite a number of heretics at Mazerolles. I know they had meetings there in the hall of the castle and sometimes outside.' She said that this was where Bishop Imbert preached. She could not find any reference to this man in Guiraud's books but Monsieur Duvernoy discovered him for me and provided me with a full dossier about him.[2]

She found from Guiraud that the de Mazerolles and de Lauracs were intermarried. 'Blanche de Laurac, Helis, Fabrissa de Mazerolles are all related.' Helis is the Alaïs referred to by Mrs. Smith quite early in this book. She, as Puerilia, was constantly with Hélis and Fabrissa. At this point it is best to state clearly that Mrs. Smith's main contentions are absolutely correct. Helis was Roger's sister and Pierre de Mazerolles' mother. She was also Fabrissa's sister-in-law. Further evidence of the identity of these characters will be given in a later section.

On April 18th she expressed disappointment with her brief and rapid perusal of Guiraud. My own was not much better. At this stage of the proceedings I seem to have lost interest. It is difficult to explain why I did not make, at this time, a concentrated rush to establish my previous identity. It is remarkable how much I missed in Guiraud's book when I skipped through it for the first time. Certainly I did not set myself to read it as a whole. At the back of my mind was the idea that if things are to be revealed they will be revealed.

Mrs. Smith's disappointment with Guiraud had a specific

[2] See later.

origin. She was looking all the time for a reference to Grisolles because she had known Roger by this surname.

There is again a slip back into an ambivalent attitude to the whole experience. 'At the root of it all, I'm afraid. Afraid a Roger de Grisolles will turn up in some records somewhere, because then I'll be forced to accept that this man did exist. You can see I'm very mixed up at the moment.'

26

There was a further communication dated the 19th April. Something happened which caused Mrs. Smith to panic. I thought it was a small affair compared with the previous experiences she had undergone. She had thought previously all her father's family were dead but 'Not long ago a woman called on my mother and said she was a companion to my great aunt who is dying. I've never known about my grandmother's family except that they once lived at Ashridge, but this woman told us that my great grandparents were French. All were devout Catholics.' Mrs. Smith added, 'I do get a little apprehensive about what might turn up next. It's a bit uncanny.' In a subsequent letter she added that her mother had said the day previously that her father had never breathed a word about his grandparents being French. It appears that one of her grandmother's brothers was a Roman Catholic priest. She only discovered later that the family name was French, with in fact a quite positive similarity to my own.

I saw her on April 24th. She produced a series of photographs of herself taken when she was younger. Allowing for photographs taken at different ages, her face, as revealed in these quite good snapshots, had such a capacity to change that, had I not been told beforehand that she was the subject, I could have said that the photographs were not of the same person. I have often noticed this extreme variability of countenance in psychic people. Perhaps it is merely that past personalities show up easier in them than in others.

On April 24th she wrote to the effect that whereas in the past she had often been depressed and unhappy, she had recently been exceptionally contented. She said she supposed peace of mind would be achieved when one learnt to accept life's disciplinary experiences, problems and heartaches. She said she felt better equipped to help others and more tolerant.

On the 29th she received a letter from a Roman Catholic priest in Scotland whom she had never met and who was a relative of her grandfather's generation. He said he was fascinated by the subject of his ancestors and had traced the family back to the Middle Ages in Florence. The latter city was at one time a stronghold of Catharism.

Towards the end of May she told me that she had heard from a friend of hers in France that there was land for sale in the neighbourhood of Grisolles and that people were reluctant to buy it. The land in question was believed to be a Cathar burial ground and said to be haunted by the Cathars. Her friend's brother took a chance on the land, made an offer for it as he considered it might be useful to him in his business, but for a time could find nobody willing to sign the agreement. In an article by Monsieur Duvernoy I discovered that there were only three Cathar burial grounds which we know of with any certainty. I dismissed the matter as a local superstition. Then in April 1969 I discovered from a re-reading of Guiraud that the Seigneurs of Montesquieu were ardent Cathars and that different generations of the family were interred in a burial ground in that vicinity. I found from the map that Montesquieu was, like Grisolles, only a few miles from Toulouse, though south of that city. I asked Mrs. Smith to write to her friend in France to see whether the land in question which her friend's brother had had so much difficulty in buying was situated at Montesquieu. She replied in a letter received by me on May 3rd that this was not so. The tone of her letter was to the effect that she was sorry to disappoint me. She did not do so. She described the land, now in the

111

possession of her friend, as at a place called Muret. She was afraid this point would not add any interest to the narrative. But emphatically it does.

Muret is situated a short distance to the south of Toulouse. It is the site of de Montfort's crowning victory which destroyed for ever the hope of freedom for the Languedoc and toleration for the Cathar faith. The army of the Count of Toulouse had been reinforced by that of King Pierre of Aragon. Due to a fatuous disregard of tactics and ordinary caution on the part of the latter the advantage of superiority in numbers was thrown away. Pierre of Aragon was himself killed and there was considerable slaughter among the armies of the Languedoc. Though hostilities were resumed more than once in the next score of years, Muret was the real graveyard of the Cathar hopes. It may not have been an actual cemetery in the accepted sense of the word, though thousands of Cathars and their supporters must have been interred there. Certainly in the metaphorical sense it fulfilled the description. One wonders whether the site of land ultimately purchased by the brother of Mrs. Smith's friend actually included a portion of the battlefield.

On May 28th she said that she recalled, in a dream, the coins she carried when she went to Fabrissa. She made a drawing of them—they were all of the same kind—and sent it along with the letter. I know nothing of numismatics and can draw no firm conclusions from this coin but, like all the questions raised by Mrs. Smith, it is of great interest and merits discussion.

The next day, May 29th, I received from Mrs. Smith the following description of this particular coin. 'The coins weren't perfectly round, and were slightly smaller than the one I've tried to draw here. You know I'm not much of an artist, but I'm pretty sure I've got the lettering right, as I made a note of it the moment I woke up. The writing does not mean much to me—it doesn't look like French or Latin does it? On the reverse side is a man's head—not in profile, but full face, but I can't possibly draw that I'm afraid. I know it seems ridiculous but some of the coins were cut in half—I'm certain of that.'

Drawing of coin from Mrs. Smith's dream

Later she recalled a further point about the coins. 'One point I forgot to mention about the coins, and that is that they didn't have a date on them! Perhaps then they came under the heading of token coinage, for don't you think all the official ones would bear a date? Also, I wouldn't like to say for certain that the man's head on the reverse side is that of a king, because he isn't shown wearing a crown. Just a young man with shoulder length hair.'

My comments are as follows. Firstly she did not realise that cutting coins in half was common practice in the Middle Ages. She corrected this later. She made enquiries from a friend who collected. She discovered that halving the coins was a common practice because they were usually silver and worth the amount of silver they weighed.

As to the identification of this particular coin her friend pointed out that in the thirteenth century France, unlike England, did not have a single unified coinage and that there were many feudal issues. I do not think it necessary to labour the diversity of French coinage in the thirteenth century. The Languedoc must inevitably have had its own coinage. It represented a distinct and autonomous civilisation. Any vassalage exhibited towards the kings of France was more or less nominal until, of course, the situation was altered by the Crusades against the Albigensians.

The head on the other side of the coin could have been that of one of the Counts of Toulouse. As it was that of a young man,

113

and if the coin had been minted fairly recently before Puerilia carried it in her sack, it could also have been the head of Raymond-Roger Trencavel, Vicomte of Carcassonne and Bezières, protector of heretics, who died, or was murdered by the Crusaders, in his late twenties in his own castle at Carcassonne.

I cannot comment on Mrs. Smith's query that the official ones should surely have borne a date.

Her friend suggested that this coin might be an example of an official issue struck in a time of emergency, like a siege. The time of which we are writing was certainly a period of crisis. There were sieges in plenty, Toulouse, Fanjeaux, Montréal, Carcassonne, Minerve, Termes, etc. Puerilia herself had taken part in one. Mrs. Smith's friend was very interested in the coin and asked to see it if it was in her possession. Mrs. Smith commented, 'I don't know her well enough to say I only dreamt about it. Obviously I want to find out more, but the "experts" get too curious and I'm still sensitive about telling anyone.'

On June 10th, 1966, she wrote asking me if, should I still have her letter, I could examine it and see if the lettering on the coin looked anything like Figeac. She could not find the scrap of paper on which she had made her sketch of the coin. She said, 'I seem to remember there was a letter F but I haven't a clue about the rest of it. The lettering was so strange. Anyway, what I am getting at is this.

'Someone told me this week there is an interesting mediaeval town in France, somewhere in the region of Albi, called Figeac. She said it was a town well worth a visit and a former thirteenth-century mint. Have you ever heard of this town?'

Figeac exists. It is even the birthplace of Charles Boyer. There is something like an F in the drawing of the coin. I could not discover anything approximating to the name Figeac or to any Latin version of it. But why should a coin bear the name Figeac merely because it was minted there? Figeac must have been too small a place in the Middle Ages to produce a coinage merely for its own use.

An inquiry at the Department of Coins and Medals at the

British Museum confirmed that a mint at Figeac was opened for Philip VI in 1346. It also struck coins for Edward the Black Prince of Aquitaine. As the mint at Figeac was not opened till a century after the death of Roger it is not relevant to our story.

The identity of Mrs. Smith's coin is a matter for the experts. It is more satisfying to hear from her a piece of first-hand evidence from the thirteenth century. 'We didn't use an awful lot of money in those days. We mostly lived by exchanging goods. Since the Church was so keen on confiscating goods, it is quite likely that people such as the Cathars who were constantly being persecuted and often had to leave places in a hurry, should convert anything they possessed into silver and the like, which could be carried away and hidden if necessary. A great advantage of having silver coins was that they could be melted down and used for making other items and the value of the silver remained the same. The buckle of the Parfait's girdle was silver, and the only thing of value they personally possessed. Perhaps I shouldn't write as positively as this. After all, these are only dreams. I make no claim to being right and I am not an authority on the Middle Ages. I'm always afraid I might mislead you with details I give you.'

In putting the final touches to this book I wrote again to Mrs. Smith on the subject of this coin. In a letter dated May 20th, 1969, she wrote, 'Coins, I should think it O.K. to mention them but I wouldn't try to do a section on it because this is something I'm not 100 per cent sure about. As I've told you before, I have collected and studied coins and because of this one can never be sure if what I've drawn isn't simply a sub-conscious memory of something I've read over the years. True, I've not read a very great deal on the subject and I know nothing whatsoever about pre-eighteenth century coins, but I must be honest because this is a hobby of mine.'

I quote this letter to show Mrs. Smith's conscientious and highly self-critical attitude towards her own dreams and memories. The reader may agree with her in minimising the value of what she says about the coin. I myself definitely regard it as evidence, simply because to disregard anything she says is foolish because she has been so often right. Also it seems to me that, in view of her clear memories of Fabrissa, Roger, Helis and Pierre, we should pay serious attention to her possibly extremely vivid recollection of the coin she was carrying on her journey to Fabrissa. After all, this was one of the crucial periods in her life. As Roger said, 'If anything happens to me go to Fabrissa.' Nevertheless, though I classified her recollection of the coin as admissible evidence, I did not regard it as a striking contribution. There was, however, something more to be said on the subject. As we shall see on page 119 Professor Nelli had further contributions to make.

There then followed a period of several weeks during which I had little to record. During July Mrs. Smith spent a good deal of time writing to different sources in France to see if she could identify Roger de Grisolles. She failed to do so. She had one communication which might have been of importance. On the 19th she said that she received a letter from a student in Castelnaudary. The latter said that Roger de Grisolles was probably a childhood nickname of a friend of a family of heretics from Mazerolles. Mrs. Smith replied with a great number of questions but received no answer and furthermore lost the address of her informant.[1] Later the idea came to me that Grisolles was not the name of a place, though such a place exists, but the description of a characteristic of the man concerned. In my dictionary I found that the verb grisoller meant to warble like a lark. I was very pleased with what I regarded as a flash of intuition. As Guiraud and the depositions before the Inquisitors make clear, Roger, as a member of the Fanjeaux family, belonged to a very active group of Cathar nobility in the neighbourhood of Fanjeaux, Montréal and Mazerolles. These families were considerably intermarried. They included the Durforts, whose family name was Feste. Roger was the grandson of Guillaume de Durfort. The latter was, according to Professor Nelli, whose standards are very strict, the

[1] It is unfortunate that Mrs. Smith lost track of this young man. I should dearly love to know why he regarded the name of Grisolles as a nickname.

only recognised troubadour who was indubitably a practising Cathar. One is entitled to wonder whether, in such an *ambience*, Roger had aspirations to be a troubadour. We have absolutely definite evidence on this point. One cannot say that he wrote poetry but he was always singing and reciting it. Mrs. Smith recalls some of these poems. They are quoted and discussed in a later section. Is it fanciful to imagine that in such a setting, and with such poetic and musical interests, Roger should have acquired a nickname derived from the verb to sing like a lark?

Sometime in July, the letter was undated, I heard something of Roger's temperament. Mrs. Smith said she knew very little about me—she obviously found me stiff and formal—and such a lot about Roger. 'Roger was like a small boy at times.' She had to be everything to him and also, 'the object of his temper when he felt grumpy. He needed a sympathetic ear, someone to listen to his ideas, his hopes, dreams, woes and troubles. He was inclined to be jealous too, entirely without cause. He was a little arrogant, possibly a little conceited, and liked to get his own way.' By way of compensation he appears to have been of some use to the suffering. It is positively depressing, but I cannot see that I have changed a great deal over seven hundred years. In a later letter dated September 15th she reverts to the same theme. 'Roger, without being aware of it, had very definite ideas of how people should live and behave, and often he tried to mould them into being as he wished. I'm afraid he didn't always succeed.'

27

On September 5th I received a letter from her prior to her setting off with her husband on a holiday to France. She asked to be reassured that it was all right for her to go to Toulouse. She telephoned later for further reassurance.

On, I think, September 10th she wrote a letter in which she said that the night previously she had the strange impression that 'I was looking at myself. I felt as if I was standing by the bed holding someone's hand. He seemed to be talking to me for a long time and I felt peaceful listening to him. I can't remember much of what he said, but it wasn't Roger, because during this strange conversation he told me his father was in India. His voice sounded like yours, but I wasn't aware of what he looked like.' My father left for India when I was about seven and stayed there for some years. Mrs. Smith was quite unaware of this.

At the end of her letter she hoped that she might have a quiet spell during her impending holiday. She said that if she started remembering too much she ran a high temperature and developed a severe headache. I do not know about the high temperature but the headache is interesting and perfectly in order. A proportion of cases of migraine are attributable to psychic factors. I have learnt a good deal as to the origin of disease from Mrs. Smith and others like her.

I had a communication dated September 13th from France. She had not had, after all, to go through Toulouse because the road to that city was blocked. It was as though the fates were interfering on her behalf, protecting her from the city and sending her instead through Pamiers and Foix, in fact along a road which had been incessantly used by the Cathars.

A further letter said that she had seen Professor Nelli's latest book, *Le Musée du Catharisme*. 'In it there is a drawing of a disc-shaped stele like this

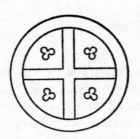

Stele with design resembling Mrs. Smith's coin

which appears to have the same design as the coin I mentioned,[2] but without the lettering. I wish I could be absolutely certain of the latter. The trouble is that when I am sufficiently wide awake to take a pencil to draw, I find it difficult to remember the exact shape and order of the letters.' She added later, 'I am rather ignorant on the subject of mystical symbols.'

In putting the final touches to this book I thought it worth while to send a copy of Mrs. Smith's rough drawing of the coin to Professor Nelli. I had a letter from him on July 3rd, 1969. He claimed no knowledge of coinage but said that the design on the coin in question could be Cathar. It resembles more than one of the steles and decorative themes illustrated in his book *Le Musée de Catharisme*.

I obtained still more positive evidence about this coin on October 3rd, 1969, when I visited the Museum at Toulouse with Monsieur Duvernoy. We found coins with a definite likeness to that drawn by Mrs. Smith. There were two main features in common. Several of the coins in the museum were like Mrs. Smith's, divided into four. Secondly, we found specimens with the same small crosses as those depicted by her. As in her drawing the crosses were placed in equal numbers in each quarter of the coins. We could not find an example in which only one cross was placed in each quarter. These coins were quite clearly classified as emanating from Toulouse in the twelfth century. This is sound enough evidence. As Roger and Puerilia were living in the early part of the thirteenth century in the realm of the Count of Toulouse, it is only to be expected that, as at any other period in history, they used currency from the previous century.

The number of twelfth- and thirteenth-century coins in the museum was necessarily restricted. One could not expect otherwise after a lapse of eight and seven centuries. That we should have found such a degree of similarity is more than significant. We also found a limited number of coins depicting men's heads but not on those where the design on the reverse side most resembled that in Mrs. Smith's coin.

[2] In a previous letter.

In her undated letter of the latter half of September 1966 Mrs.
Smith said she was so glad that their route was diverted because
in passing through Montgaillard, just south of Foix, she remembered quite distinctly that she used to live there. 'The name itself
doesn't register with me, but the countryside was quite familiar.
Just along the road there used to be a church—an odd building
where there weren't any seats for the congregation.[1] There is a
church there now—a typical rather ugly looking country church
not a bit like the one I remember. Nearby there used to be a
place called Montbrun, but it isn't on the map anymore.' (There
are two Montbruns in the neighbourhood of Toulouse but she
regards this one as different.) 'It was *never* very big, but we
held meetings there.' Any hamlet can disappear in the course of
seven hundred years. In addition one should remember that
many were destroyed by de Montfort and his followers and
never rebuilt.

'Where did I live with Roger? Unfortunately I remember
more about life inside his house than outside, but I went to
Grisolles and I didn't feel as if I knew the place at all. The
countryside around Grisolles didn't seem hilly or wooded enough,
and the little mountain flowers I used to pick weren't growing
there. They were at Montgaillard because I found one—mauvey
pink with four petals. I picked one in the hope that I'd be able
to press it and identify it when I came home—' She asked if I
would be able to recognise it from the fragile remains. It appeared
to me to be some kind of cranesbill.

She was concerned because Grisolles did not strike a chord.
It may have been that she expected too much. She had learnt
that if one looks for experiences they do not happen. She asked,

---

[1] This is the second time Mrs. Smith has revealed her ignorance of the fact
that in the Middle Ages there was no seating accommodation for the people
in church.

'Is it at all possible in that day and age that Roger, although called de Grisolles and probably born there, could have set up an establishment further south?' The answer is that nothing could be more likely. At that time even the minor nobility had bits of land scattered about in various places. This practice seems to have been especially common in the Languedoc. She said that when she left his house she walked to Mazerolles and that it took a long time. 'I very much doubt if I could have walked from as far away as Grisolles. I know the de Mazerolles didn't all stay at Mazerolles, but Grisolles to Montgaillard seems an awfully long way for Roger to travel, although he went on horseback. Why don't I dream this in some sensible order instead of little disconnected episodes? It's so frustrating.'

Again Mrs. Smith underestimates the distances covered by people in the Middle Ages and does not make allowance for the fact that the Cathars were notoriously great travellers. With regard to Montgaillard, I thought I had discovered a solution to her problem. There is a place of that name in the Corbières, in the wild hill country of the Eastern Pyrenees, situated not too far from Mazerolles. Unfortunately Mrs. Smith persists that the Montgaillard she knew was that in the vicinity of Foix. Certainly, it is a place of significance in the Cathar story because Pierre-Roger de Mirepoix retired there after the fall of Montségur where he had been commander of the garrison.[1]

She confided to a French woman friend that she had been dreaming about life in the Middle Ages. Her friend was not at all surprised and said that she had read and heard of this sort of thing before and had some experience of it herself. I was not surprised at this statement because, in psychic matters, like attracts like even though one may be unaware for a long time that one's friends are so endowed.

It was on this return journey that she had lunch at Grisolles. This was neither by her choice nor suggestion. In a letter dated September 21st, describing her voyage home, she said they drove through a small village called St. Paul de Jarrat. She asserted

[1] Fernand Niel. Montségur. Lesite. Son histoire 1962, p. 236.

quite confidently, 'They must have renamed it, because it used to be Montbrun.'

She then referred to her visit to Montségur. She said she heard a dove. Her husband said she imagined it but her son heard it too. 'Then, when we were sitting on the grass outside (the chateau) before descending, two doves were singing beautifully and this time all the family heard it, although we couldn't see birds at all.' The dove was a Cathar symbol. Of all the so-called Cathar relics still in existence, that of a dove in some kind of metal is regarded by Professor Nelli as among the few positively authentic relics.

She described Montségur as the most peaceful and beautiful part of France she had ever visited. 'I'd like to spend the rest of my days there.' My own reaction to Montségur—I have seen it three times and it is now two years and a half since I last visited it—is that I have never seen anywhere like it and that its beauty has a haunting quality that I have never known elsewhere. I also had the same feeling as Mrs. Smith about wanting to stay in the chateau.

In a letter on October 2nd she again asked me to find out from Professor Nelli if Cathar priests ever wore blue. She said that both Rogers wore blue and also some of the other men at the meeting. She says, 'Certainly the women wore black at the sort of convent place where I stayed for a while and no jewellery but the girdle, if one could call that jewellery.'

Now here we come to the end of the blue versus black controversy. On August 24th 1969 I read in Professor Nelli's latest book La Vie Quotidienne des Cathares, that Cathar priests always wore black until the times of persecution, following which, by way of disguise, they often switched over to dark blue. This absolutely confirms Mrs. Smith's contentions both as to colour and period. All her recollections are of the times of persecution during and between the Albigensian wars and at the time of the Inquisition. They are concerned with the first half of the thirteenth century or, more specifically, with the period from the 1220s to the early 1240s. It is fascinating and appropriate that

I should have read this culminating statement as to the colour of the robes of the Cathar priests in a work by Professor Nelli. It is over four years ago since this erudite and extremely meticulous authority told me, in expressing his astonishment at the accuracy of Mrs. Smith's recollections, that when in doubt I should go by the patient.

Speaking of my intending holiday she wondered if 'you'll get to Montgaillard and if the place will mean anything to you. I wandered along past the houses and into the countryside and it was like returning home after years away'. She reverted again to the fact that her going to Montgaillard was, as it were, accidental because of the road block at Toulouse. 'At Montgaillard I felt ridiculously happy because there I felt close to Roger. I've fashioned my life on his teaching and it is essential that I have faith in my dreams.'

She then went on to describe further the character of Roger. I have certain identical traits. She said that Roger had a passion for being out of doors. Passion in no exaggerated description for my own love of the open air. Frequently people have asked where I have been for my holiday when, in actual fact, I have not been away. My tan has been acquired, even in the most mediocre summers, from my habit of seeing patients for hours in the open air. I simply loathe being inside a house on a summer day. Roger felt at peace in the countryside. When I was younger I had a passion for the country. This is less than it was but is still considerable. I do not think I exaggerate if I say that I am very close to nature. Roger was also not very practical. He left the business side of the management of his house to his sister. I performed this identical tactic with my wife. I am also equally hopeless at repairs. She points out also a similarity between Roger and myself. 'You were both the type to get things done for you without too many requests, fuss or argument.' She attributed this to the fact that both Roger and I had a capacity to look helpless. She was good enough to say that this was not 'a deliberate pose but the manner you were born with'. I must admit I have never lacked people who were willing to help me.

Talking about prayer she said that she did not pray very often but that when she did she was frequently helped and guided. She said that at the age of fifteen she doubted the existence of God and 'I prayed for—no, demanded—proof, and got it. It made me very afraid at the time but I was taught a valuable lesson and I found a faith I'll never lose.' She did not specify what was the proof she was given or what was the nature of the lesson she was taught. She said that very often when she offered prayers, which she tended only to do when she was desperate, the latter were granted. She did not say to what degree her requests in prayer were for something specific.

Referring again to her visit to Montségur she said that, like me, she had a fear that she might experience a feeling of horror but that when she arrived there she found only peace.

29

During October my wife and I went for a holiday to France. We visited Montségur. In the late afternoon and evening of late autumn it was more beautiful than ever. We visited the little museum in the village. It contained a number of coins and jetons with signs which could have been Manichæen. I am afraid I did not study them very closely. My interest in the Cathars has, at the conscious level, waxed and waned, though I feel an unswerving loyalty to them and would always arise to combat their detractors. But in addition I am by no means research minded or a natural scholar. My impatience with detail has been a handicap to me in many ways, including the putting together of this book.

Something interesting happened within an hour of arriving at Carcassonne. I went out with a friend for a cup of tea while the rest of the party stayed in the hotel. An elderly man was sitting at a table. I certainly registered his face, felt some kind of vague, partial recognition but did not truly recognise him. When we left the café my friend, a Catholic, commented on the beauty of his face. I responded to her comment by looking at the wrong man. Outside the café I came to the conclusion that I thought I knew him. By this time I had really recognised him as Monsieur Deodat Roché, whom I had encountered previously and whom I have mentioned before as one of the greatest living interpreters of Catharism. My companion was insistent that I return, which I did. He asked me to telephone him. I failed to do so but later, when we visited the small town in which he lives, I saw him again. On this occasion he showed us drawings of Cathar, Manichæen and Rosicrucian symbols. These were similar to my visionary crosses as shown below.

Either in Monsieur Rochés notes or in the museum at Montsegur, I saw something like the sign on the Parfait's buckle which so tormented Mrs. Smith.

I mention the seemingly trivial incident of my failing to recognise Monsieur Roché because I have an extraordinarily good memory for faces, which is the compensation given me by nature for an inability to remember people's names. Had Monsieur Roché been of less importance to me I would have recognised him with certainty. It was another case of raising up obstacles to enlightenment. I should also have paid far more attention to the notes he showed me.

Early in November Mrs. Smith told me that one of her daughters sometimes finished off her dreams for her. Recently she had been dreaming of Roger undergoing torture. Her youngest daughter woke her from her own nightmare by crying out in one of her own, 'They are doing something awful to Dr. Guirdham.' Such an exchange of thought and feeling in dreams, between two persons, is recognised as occurring but is by no means common. I may say that I have scarcely exchanged half a dozen words with the daughter.

In another letter Mrs. Smith mentioned briefly the tortures to which Roger was subjected. For some reason or other water was thrown over him. More orthodox treatment involved the wrenching off of his thumbs.

On November 4th Mrs. Smith stated in a letter that she used to think reincarnation was for people who had led bad lives and who were obliged to return 'to right the wrongs of the past and make a fresh start'. She now believed that some people have to come back because the world needs them to fight the forces of evil.

There is a diminution of activity until the beginning of 1967 in the early weeks of which more was happening than I noticed at the time. Mrs. Smith was very pleased that I had supplied her with the date of the attack on the Inquisitors. She said, 'I wrote to several people last year in an effort to trace Roger and the prison where he died but my chief obstacle was that I couldn't be specific about dates. Roger must have been alive in 1242.' She did not make clear why she fixed on this latter date.

Referring to the de Mazerolles puzzle, she said, 'I wish I could remember more. In the pages of notes I made years ago I didn't write much about him, but twice mentioned that Roger had known him for a long time.' (That this must have been so is quite evident from the historical records I will examine shortly.) Mrs. Smith continued, ' "Murder", I wrote "is a terrible crime but so much more terrible and shocking when carried out by someone you've known and trusted." '

She now recalled that Imbert was a Cathar bishop, 'a saintly character who was burnt to death.' Mrs. Smith was wrong in describing him as a Bishop. As we shall see later Imbert was a veritable Parfait but not a Bishop. The number of Cathar bishops

126

was minimal. 'He wore a ring like Roger but was always dressed in black—a loose garment with no girdle and no buckle. Savaric or Savarin was much more worldly. He knew the places to avoid, and places of safety, etc. "Imbert" I wrote "never gave a thought to safety. Death was his shadow and he was calm and unafraid. Florent (?) and Fabrissa saw him die and he never uttered a sound. He died as quietly and unobtrusively as he had lived."' Mrs. Smith then said, 'When I've a moment I'll try to have another go at my shorthand notes but it will take a lot of time and patience.'

It was not until January 9th, 1967, that Mrs. Smith unearthed further evidence from her notes about Imbert.[1] She describes an occasion when he stayed with Arnaud de Mazerolles. I discovered from Monsieur Duvernoy in March 1969 that the Parfait Raimond Imbert stayed at Gaja about 1210.[2] Gaja was one of the main properties of the Mazerolles family. According to Monsieur Duvernoy Imbert met Fabrissa de Mazerolles in the company of her sister-in-law Helis. It does not require any powers of deduction to prove Mrs. Smith's statement that Imbert stayed with Arnaud de Mazerolles. The latter was, after all, Helis' husband and Fabrissa's brother.

Considering the lapse of time since he lived a great deal is known about Mrs. Smith's Imbert. He was born at Moissac. He stayed at Toulouse in 1220 with Raimond Garsias and in 1228 with Pierre Mauran. He was with Pierre de Miglos at Miglos from 1227 to 1231, at Lordat about 1233, at Castellsarassin in 1239 and at Laurac in 1240-41. He preached in Fanjeaux in two houses in 1240. He is recorded as having been at Montségur in 1242. He went to Lombardy, another Cathar region, obviously to escape persecution and was seen at Asti in Italy by Bertrand de Quiders as late as 1253. His fate is described as unknown. Mrs.

[1] Till now I have followed the sequence of Mrs. Smith's letters and my notes in writing this narrative. At this stage I am changing my methods a little and rounding off all the evidence about some of the minor characters. I feel that to do so at this stage the better enables the reader to follow the narrative.
[2] This is mentioned in the deposition of Helis de Mazerolles before the Inquisitors on August 5th, 1243.

Smith has described him as dying at the stake. As she has been so right about so many things I would accept her statement.

She compares the saintly Imbert with his more worldly companion Savaric. Hear what Professor Nelli says about the latter. He describes him as a poet and an important personage. He was Seneschal of the King of England and was possibly either at Laurac or Mazerolles on the eve of the battle of Castelnaudary. One of his poems in Occitan has survived. As a man of affairs he seems to fit Mrs. Smith's description as a more worldly person and more able to look after himself.

Mrs. Smith asked where Avignonet was. She had not had time to look at the map. She asked if it was anywhere near the Montgaillard area. It is much nearer the Montgaillard I discovered in the Corbières than to the Montgaillard she had recollected when she visited it. She asked also where Pierre de Mazerolles went after the murder and if he was caught and punished. The answer is given later in the chapter on this gentleman.

She then appended as an addition to her letter a description of Pierre de Mazerolles she had just discovered among her papers in the loft. 'He was tall and might have been described as handsome but for his florid complexion and fleshy lips. He had murdered someone and was clearly stimulated by it, but the veneer of excitement couldn't hide his fear. He was afraid. I'm sure he was. We were listening to him, paying attention to every word he uttered and that pleased him very much. Pity, fear, contempt and horror—these feelings engulfed me all at once. I thought I had stopped breathing. Very carefully I inhaled and exhaled, making a conscious effort to do so. These unnatural labours brought about a dizziness that was frightening and uncontrollable, but normal breathing was difficult.' Further on she wrote, 'I had been sleeping fully clothed on the floor in the hall when I saw him (P. de Mazerolles) standing by my side, almost naked. He was horribly scarred and the top of one of his fingers was missing. His laugh was not normal. He wasn't sane at that moment. He couldn't have been. I should have pleaded with him' (elsewhere she has pointed out that he tried to kiss her)

128

'reasoned with him or prayed, but fear was in command. It hadn't robbed me of my voice though. "Roger" I shouted, and then I screamed and screamed.' Off and on in her nightmares she has continued to shout 'Roger'.

In another letter she said she could not say for certain that Pierre de Mazerolles was a relative of Fabrissa but 'if he wasn't why did we know him and why were we so upset that he was such a swine? There were dozens more like him and their behaviour didn't trouble us much. All I know about him from the maddeningly brief and sketchy notes I made years ago was: —

(a) He didn't give a damn for either Cathars or Catholics. Money was his chief interest.
(b) He was tall, dark and cruel, and was certainly the chap who terrified me in the nightmares. He was highly delighted that he had murdered someone.'

These traits in de Mazerolles' character are revealed clearly in the deposition before the Inquisition, which illustrates the cupidity and feverish vulgarity of the executioners of the Inquisitors.

At this time Mrs. Smith was still not clear as to 'who was murdered or when or where'. She did say, however, that her notes set the whole thing down in the early part of the thirteenth century.

In another letter about this time, but undated, she draws out a map to help identify the disappeared Montbrun[3] in which she is interested. The map is as follows and the site of Montbrun is somewhere in the area enclosed by the dotted lines.

Referring to her absence of any feeling of recognition about Grisolles, she said that on her visit to France she wished to go to

[3] Where Roger used to preach. To be distinguished from Montbrun (Departement Aude), see page 149.

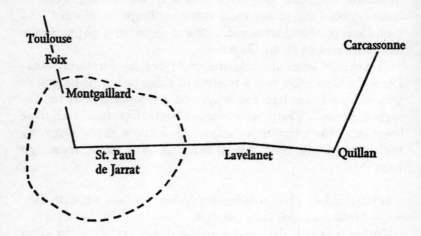

Toulouse

Foix

Carcassonne

Montgaillard

St. Paul
de Jarrat

Lavelanet

Quillan

Mazerolles because she remembered it so clearly. (I do not know if she is allowing sufficiently for the almost total disappearance of any vestiges of the thirteenth century but I feel that if she went there, in spite of the lapse of time, the place would prove familiar to her.) She then produced something very interesting. 'Somewhere near (Mazerolles) there was a place where I stayed with a lot of other women. They were all rather religious and prayed a lot and I see in the notes I made years ago that I described it as a convent. But I'm not sure that it could have been. We all wore black, but I don't know how I obtained admission because I wasn't a virgin and there were married women in the place too. The establishment was strictly a female one. Perhaps the other women were widows but there were a lot of them. In the main hall behind the raised dais there was an entrance to the quarters where the virgins slept and received instruction. We all met for meals and a prayer and after evening prayers there was a strange kissing ritual. The woman who seemed to be in charge of the place knelt down and every one of the virgins kissed her on the forehead and said something in Latin (or at least it sounded like Latin).[4] Then the rest of us all

130

knelt down and the woman who had just been kissed came to each one of us and kissed us on the forehead. A most peculiar ceremony and I don't know what the significance of it was.'

My comments on the above are as follows. There were Cathar houses, run somewhat like convents, where women were instructed in the Cathar faith. These were, as Mrs. Smith says, inhabited largely by widows and virgins. That she herself was admitted is not surprising in view of the fact that the Cathars were notoriously tolerant and charitable, in addition to which she had been the friend of one who was obviously at least very active in the Cathar faith. That there were a lot of widows in the place is not surprising in those tragic times. That the house contained also a number of married women is quite in order. Women became Parfaits, with the consent of their husbands, after raising their families.

I wrote to Professor Nelli, quoting Mrs. Smith's last mentioned letter. He said that she had provided an accurate description of Cathar ceremonial and suggested that in the future one should go by the patient's recollections of these matters.

In a letter, again undated but either at the end of December, 1966 or the beginning of January, 1967, she said, 'I can see this business of the Cathars having a simple faith seems to bother you.[5] I've read very little on the subject and I, too, see it through the mind of a peasant, probably an uneducated one. Basically their beliefs were very complicated indeed and also the preachers varied in the things they taught and talked about. But the majority of the Cathars were poor simple folk. Complicated dogma would not have been understood by them, and discussions of a more serious nature were left to the educated ones and the thinkers. The others were simply content to lead a good life, helping others and obeying simple rules of decent behaviour. They won many followers merely by their example, for the Roman Church compared most unfavourably because of the

[4] It is just possible that this was the Langue d'oc, which is nearer than French to Latin.
[5] I had asked her if she had any recollection of Cathar beliefs.

131

wealth, corruption and evil amongst the clergy and higher authorities of the Roman Church.'

In giving this description Mrs. Smith is absolutely accurate. Guiraud and other authorities make it perfectly clear that the Parfaits preached simply for the simple and retained their complex philosophy for the elect.

There is no doubt that the theology of Catharism was extremely complex and in its way as difficult to comprehend as orthodox Christian philosophy. There were two main varieties of Dualism, the mitigated and the absolute, but by the thirteenth century, Languedocien Catharism had opted decisively for the latter. What she remembers of the goodness of the lives of the Bonshommes is borne out by all the evidence, even that of the Inquisitors. The latter regarded the purity of the Parfaits as something to be used against them, believing that, because it was associated with heresy, it must necessarily be classified as hypocrisy. Evidence for the corruption of the Roman Church at that time is adequately provided by Pope Innocent the Third, who instigated the great crusade against the Albigensians but had no illusions about the failure of his own priests. Certainly Catharism must have largely spread by example and emanation but this is not really the whole story. How did it come that a creed which seems, to many modern students, to have been austere and pessimistic—I am sure it was neither—spread with such rapidity in the Languedoc and in the Midi generally, where the standard of tolerance, sophistication, learning and luxury was higher than elsewhere in Europe? Certainly it was not aided in its great and rapid spread by a complex theology. One factor is, I think, consistently overlooked. In the Middle Ages people were dominated by the fear of Hell. Catharism to some extent dissipated this fear. If the world was regarded as being made by, or under the domination of, Satan, it followed that one was entitled to regard this life as Hell. Considering that one got through it somehow, and that there were many compensations in the sunshine of the Languedoc and the Midi, the idea that the world was Hell was really an optimistic one. If this

132

world is the worst Hell one has to put up with, it must have been, even at its lowest, vastly preferable to the perpetual damnation of the orthodox Christians of that epoch.

Mrs. Smith said that Roger went off meditating on his own and that she never asked him about his beliefs. Though she lived with him, she 'had to pay him a certain amount of respect like all the others and I wouldn't have thought it proper to question him about what he thought, where he went, or what he did.' This is reasonable enough. The simple croyant was supposed to go on his knees on meeting a Parfait, an act of respect described as 'adoration'. Not that I think that Roger was a Parfait but he certainly seems, with his preaching, his garb and his meditations, to have been qualifying for the rôle. Also, as I discovered later, he was very much older than she was.

There is an interesting letter from her on November 17th on the nature of good and evil. 'The difference between something bad and something evil is, to my way of thinking, the effect it has on others.' She goes on to say that she certainly believes 'that light and darkness, good and evil, exist with independent powers side by side'. She does not classify bad, immoral or mean actions as evil if people are not irrevocably hurt by them. 'I would,' she said, 'describe as evil someone who uses the powers of his mind to destroy others. When I encounter evil my peace of mind is instantly shattered and I react with a feeling of intense loathing and mental agitation. Mind you, I don't always feel calm and peaceful in the presence of good, but I do feel fortified by it.' These ideas are in part Dualist because she recognises goodness and evil as energies. She is also harking back to primitive Christianity which spread by emanation.

30

On January 8th, 1967 I received a letter in which she again mentions St. Papoul. She said that the second Roger was captured there but added that as far as she could see the place does not exist. Her self-critical faculty leads her to say that perhaps she made up the name years ago but that it seems unlikely. St. Papoul very certainly exists and to this day. It was the scene of an incident involving the Cathars recorded by Monsieur Duvernoy in an article in Cahiers du Sud.

Referring to her search for Grisolles in Guiraud's *History of the Inquisition*, she pointed out that she ignored the references to Mazerolles. She said 'the de Mazerolles names should have stuck out like a sore thumb, but they didn't register with me at all. I can't think why, except perhaps that most of my life I set up a mental block when there are names and places I don't want to remember.' As I have said, all through my life I have reacted likewise. So far as the de Mazerolles are concerned, as I indicated previously I spent a good deal of time tracing them in Guiraud and elsewhere when, in actual fact, I had read about them first in Zoë Oldenbourg's popular work and long before Mrs. Smith had mentioned their name.

She said that writing had always been a solace to her and a way of 'getting things out of her system'. She said that it was impossible to tell twenty years later how much was added as 'padding for the novel' and how much was exact description of the dreams. She added, 'The names seem strange though—Fabrissa, Imbert, Florent etc. are hardly the names a schoolgirl could choose, especially one not in the least bit interested in history, and I wasn't.' One can only completely agree. The idea that an English schoolgirl of thirteen could concoct accurately old Languedocien names is untenable. In addition she cannot invent the history of the thirteenth century. She may refer to her work as padding for the novel but the padding was pure fact and verifiable as such by consulting the historians.

134

In the same letter she said she wondered if her experience in Bayonne and St. Jean Pied de Port might be evidence of previous incarnations. She said that though she had never visited the latter place before, she knew her way around it as well as she knew her native town.

Then followed an extract from her schoolgirl notes. It refers to her life in the Cathar women's Home. 'I was glad Alaïs (Helis) said she would stay because there was no one else I knew. Later on I was sure I'd make friends among these people. They were very kind but because I was tired and Roger was no longer with me, I started to cry. They gave me something to drink and I was glad when it was time to sleep. A lot of women shared the same room and it was good to have company. Several of them dressed like nuns but they didn't have crucifixes or rosary beads.[1] I think they were some sort of religious body like Quakers,[2] and this was one of their convents. Yet the building from the outside looked like a castle.'

She then wrote, 'A lot here I can't read. It goes on, "I couldn't forget Roger and I wanted to die so that I could be reunited with him. Did all those widows secretly grieve as I did? I was often ashamed because I cried so much and then not surprisingly I became quite ill when I heard that his friend Roger had died too. With both of them gone I could never be happy again. We had been warned often enough not to go to St. Papoul so why did he ignore the advice and go there? Several others were caught when he was. It was so horrible. They were all dying."'

31

In a letter of the 9th January, 1967, Mrs. Smith deplored that she had got rid of her novel because of her dread of it when she found that it so resembled the wording of Madame X's essay. This

[1] Such decorations were anathema to the Cathars.
[2] Not a bad guess this, seeing that the Cathars, like the Quakers, were of non-resistant, pacifist inclination. They had also other resemblances to the Quakers. They would not, for example, take oaths in giving evidence.

remark was provoked by other discoveries when sorting out her papers. There was another warning from Savaric about not going to St. Papoul but the most important item in this letter was her contribution to the affair d'Adalo.

She had found several names jotted down on a piece of paper with no accompanying explanation. She had written down a name that looked like Bruseré but she did not know whether this was the name of a place or person. This name conveys nothing to me. Then she described the form of the note following the mention of this name. It was, to use her own words, 'Under a heading just like this: —

'Sicard and Guiraut
Bräida de Laurac
Roger's mother'

She said that this did not necessarily mean that the Bräida de Laurac was Roger's mother. 'They may be two different people.' Her caution is justified. Roger's mother was a lady called Aude de Tonnens. Then she goes on to say 'I don't indicate which Roger either'. As we shall see later the second Roger was called Roger de la Tour de Laurac. Bräida was the mother of the second Roger.

Now she had sent me some weeks previously a note to the effect that she had found a scrap of paper on which were written simply the same names Sicard and Guiraud together with that of de Levis. She had not the slightest idea what was the connection if any between these three people.

There is another extract from a letter written on January 10th, 1967. Roger had returned after being away for some time. She wrote, 'It was obvious to me that things had gone badly. He was nervously stroking his beard and brushing his hair with his hand, as he always did when he was worried, and I saw that he had been biting his nails again.

'Toulouse fits into this somewhere or other. I write about a house near Toulouse but apart from Alaïs and Roger, I don't

136

mention anyone else. There is a description of a battle raging near Toulouse and our heroine seems to have had an exciting time throwing stones.'

On Thursday, January 12th, there was another important letter. I will quote it pretty fully. 'With much sweat and toil I have deciphered this bit: —

'The old man (?) was going to die soon.[1] Roger had been with him for two days and he hadn't spoken. The noise of the fighting could he heard clearly and I was afraid. Life was cheap, wiped out in seconds. Soon everyone in the world would be killed and the earth strewn with rotten, stinking flesh. Roger had stayed all this time with the old man who was going to die anyway. I loved him for it but how tired he looked. "Sicard and Guiraut should be here. I will find them," I said.' The repetition of the names Sicard and Guiraud should be noted carefully. 'Roger did not want me to go but he was too weary to put up any resistance. I kissed him quietly and ran outside. He was worried I know but I was sick of doing nothing. The din was terrible. Even the men were screaming. I saw Mie (that's what the name looks like but my writing is terrible. All I can be definite about is the M and the I, the last letter could be anything.') This is not Mie but Mir, in fact Mir de Camplong who was the second of Roger's great friends. 'He was dishevelled and plastered with blood and grime but I saw him as someone good and sane in a world of madmen. I told him the old man was dying, and a woman said she had not long ago talked to the D'Adalo brothers (terrible writing again but I think that's the name.) I asked Mie to help find them. He said he had no weapons but would come with me. "Avoid trouble, if you can," he said, "but keep some stones ready and aim to kill the bastards." (Nice lot of people we mixed with.)'

It was not long before I lost him in the crowd. Sicard and Guiraud were no where to be seen either and the noise and the smell were making me feel sick. Then I was really sick when I stumbled over a man who had no feet. His nose was smashed in

[1] The question mark is Mrs. Smith's. The old man was G. d'Adalo, father of Sicard, Guiraud and Gaucerand. He was killed at the siege of Fanjeaux.

and one ear was missing. He was still alive even in that state. I joined in with the stone throwing but I didn't kill anyone. I am glad I didn't. All around were dead, wounded and mutilated bodies.' Then she added, 'Simon de Montfort is not mentioned anywhere. I don't say who we were fighting.' She puts this in because when she had previously raised the question of throwing stones in a battle I pointed out to her that this was common form and that it was always traditionally stated Simon de Montfort had been killed by a woman.

'Then comes the most revolting description of the battle scene. I am not usually squeamish but it put me off my dinner yesterday evening and I lay awake for hours last night unable to get it out of my mind. If there is any truth in the dreams, these people were demons without any vestige of human decency.'

On the 15th January, 1967 I had another letter from Mrs. Smith. It contained a passage of immense importance. 'I have been having another look at my notes. Sicard and Guiraud d'Antlo—D'Abalo—d'Adalo—d'Alfar (oh, my dreadful writing), don't seem to be connected with Avignonet in any way. I can't think why I should connect them with de Levis. The chap called Mie, Mir or Min seems to be closely connected with Roger. What queer names some of them have. The old man Roger sat with when he was dying is the father of Sicard and Guiraud d'Adalo' —she gets the spelling right this time—'if that is any help.'

In reality this is one of the most graphic and convincing pieces of evidence produced by Mrs. Smith. It is all the more interesting in that it concerns very minor characters on the stage of history but who nevertheless are still traceable owing to the ant-like industry of the Inquisitors and their clerks. Let us go back to the first reference to Sicard and Guiraud. They are mentioned alongside de Levis. This is because, with a third brother Gaucerand, they belonged to the suite of the Seigneur called de Levis. The latter was the lord of Mirepoix. He had displaced the previous owner because of the latter's undisguised fidelity to Catharism. This usurpation must, according to Monsieur Duvernoy, have occurred at least as early as 1239. In spite of their duties as part of the de Levis' entourage the brothers remained staunch Cathars. (Two took part in the defence of Montségur and one was killed there.)

And the old man, father of Guiraud and Sicard? We do not know his Christian name. He is only referred to in the records as G. d'Adalo. G seems to have been a favourite initial in the d'Adalo family. In addition to those already mentioned, two illegitimate members are recorded, both with Christian names beginning with G.

D'Adalo senior died at the siege of Fanjeaux. Mrs. Smith's graphic description is of the investment of the city. The fact that she failed to mention Simon de Montfort in her notes is another testimony to her accuracy. Simon de Montfort was killed at Toulouse in 1213.

Sicard died, having received the Consolamentum, in 1239.

We next come to a fascinating but readily soluble problem posed by Mrs. Smith's proffering of alternative names for the d'Adalo brothers. In assessing her spelling we should remember that she is recording in phonetic spelling in a foreign language words possibly heard in phrases of clairaudience. In addition, even in arriving at the name d'Adalo, we are only using the Latin version written in the Inquisitional records. As Monsieur Duvernoy pointed out in a letter, the spelling in Langue d'oc was d'Adalou. Anyway we have 'Sicard and Guiraud d'Antlo, d'Abalo, d'Adalo, d'Alfar.' If we take the first three versions our problem is simple. Mrs. Smith was right at the third attempt and d'Adalo is the usual form adopted by the historians. But what of the name d'Alfar? Should we dismiss this as another version of d'Adalo? And why the statement that these names 'don't seem to be connected to Avignonet in any way?'

If one regards the four different spellings the last d'Alfar stands out as quite different from the first three versions. It is easily conceivable that any of the first three could be mistaken for each other. But in all fairness it has to be admitted that the sound of d'Alfar is radically different. And the statement that there is no connection with Avignonet? But there is an utterly

clear and irrefutable connection. D'Alfar, or d'Alfaro, was a
different person. He was an agent of the Count of Toulouse. His
connection with Avignonet is undoubted, crucial and a matter
of history. He was the person into whose house the Inquisitors
were received before being massacred. It was intended that they
should stay the night. It was d'Alfar who arranged for the
murderers, including Pierre de Mazerolles, to be admitted to the
house. When fitted together, there is a remorseless logic in Mrs.
Smith's jigsaw pieces. What is more the reference to d'Alfar
helps all the more to pivot the story round the crucial date 1242,
the year in which the Inquisitors were massacred. Mrs. Smith has
always insisted that Roger was alive at this date.

In another letter Mrs. Smith says that Sicard and Guiraud
'must have been soldiers because they were always fighting'.
Once again she was right. They are so described in the description given by Arnaud Roger de Mirepoix before the Inquisitors in
1244.

32

In this letter of January 15th, 1967 Mrs. Smith was self-critical.
She wondered whether too much importance should be attached
to the names she used in the notes she made as a schoolgirl.
Mentioning the names Fabrissa, Bräida and Sicard she asked,
'Might there not be some logical explanation as to why I used
these names?' Whatever the explanation of this story, there is no
element of fabrication here. English schoolgirls of thirteen do not
stumble on names like Fabrissa, Braïda, Sicard and Alaïs, nor do
they string them together by some dexterous alchemy to accord
with the obscure facts of history enacted in a foreign country.

A few days later I received another letter in which she
stressed the importance of Arnaud de Mazerolles. 'I can't get
that name out of my mind and if we are lucky enough to find anyone who can say definitely that this man existed, then I shall
feel we are making headway at last.' There cannot be any doubt

about his existence. There are numerous references to him in the relevant records. His place in the de Mazerolles family and as the husband of Helis is clear beyond doubt. Apart from my perusual of the available authorities I had direct confirmatory evidence from Professor Nelli and Monsieur Duvernoy.

The letter continues, 'Once I remarked that Bishop Imbert stayed with him (i.e. Arnaud de Mazerolles) and then comes an interesting bit. It concerns Alaïs, Roger's sister. There is a lot of description which I won't bore you with. Then it goes on, I wondered how she felt about returning to Mazerolles. Alaïs never mentioned Arnaud but I am sure that she still loved him. "Why did you marry him?" I asked her. But she looked sad and said nothing.' The gist of the matter is that in becoming a Parfaite Helis ceased to lead a marital life with her husband. In saying 'Why did you marry him?' it may be that Puerilia could not understand that Helis could still be in love with her husband and yet dedicated to a life of the spirit. Or there may have been some element of disharmony between them. This is one thing we will never know.

I note that the colours under my eyes changed in January and asked myself if the brighter colours could mean happiness. There was a combination of purple with light green and also a lovely sky blue with magenta nuclei. I wondered if January is my month.

I was ill at this time. The Consultant called in happened, above all things, to have met Monsieur X and his wife. It was interesting that, true to my habit of unconsciously resisting these psychic synchronisations, I had put off seeing this Consultant but had ultimately succumbed when the general practitioner raised the question a second time and more insistently.

Going back to January 27th, in an article by Duvernoy on the Cathars and the Problem of Evil, I discovered that a certain Raymond Barth left the Leper House where he lived with his mistress to organise an attack designed to rescue two Parfaits seized by the Catholic authorities. This affair took place in the neighbourhood of St. Papoul. Going back to my Cathar novel, my hero's first love was a leper ! The Leper House was at Laurac. Was this due to some distant and buried memory of having been captured at St. Papoul? In ordinary life in situations of great agony one sometimes notes associated circumstances with piercing clarity. I wonder if the same applies to far memory at the unconscious level. Perhaps one remembers the leper house and forgets being captured.

33

Mrs. Smith said that she was very pleased that she did not throw away the school books she wrote in years ago as there was still much in them that she had forgotten.

On the 26th January I had another interesting letter from her. She said, 'I hope you don't mind getting my transcriptions in bits and pieces. The trouble is that a lot of it is mixed up with school work, other short stories, poems, etc. and it takes ages to sort it all out.'

Referring again to Mir, of whom she had spoken before, here is something more she wrote about him. 'Savaric said a meeting was due to take place at Montlaur soon. Bishop Imbert had intended to send someone else but Savaric put in a word for Mie —Mir.[1] Savaric was like that—always kind and considerate. He knew Mir had not been home since the death of his mother and Montlaur was near his home so it wouldn't take long to get there. Roger went with him, of course. It would be a long journey. I hated the times when he had to go away.'

Mrs. Smith then commented that she could not find a place called Montlaur or anything similar to it near Mirepoix. She commented that there may have been such a place years ago. She was preoccupied with Montlaur because it is written very clearly in her notes. It was important to her because this was the place near where Mir lived at the time. She pointed out that the world-famous professor she had previously consulted con-

[1] She was uncertain of the spelling of his name which was certainly Mir.

firmed that such a place existed. She need not have bothered to consult this eminent authority. Montlaur is situated in the Corbières, one of the most inaccessible and determined redoubts of Catharism. Its gentry were among those who fought longest against the Catholics from the north. Camplong, from which Roger's friend Mir derived his surname, is situated directly to the east of Montlaur and a stone's throw from it. Mrs. Smith is once again dead accurate.

34

Mrs. Smith's letter of March 31st is interesting. I suggested in a letter to her that perhaps at this stage in the decline of Western civilisation, it might help people to know that reincarnation was a fact. I suggested this only tentatively because I find it hard to accept that proselytising is ever of value, least of all in religion. Also I do not think that the concept of reincarnation, while certainly reasonable, is necessarily cheerful. There are certain moods when the 'it's all to do over again idea' is a little wearying. She said, 'I gather that you think I should at least get some satisfaction out of far memory and that it should help to know I'm right.' She then continued that to know she was right was a help but only because she no longer worried that she suffered from some form of insanity. She said, 'I suppose I could have sorted out the details of my dreams many years ago but I didn't for the simple reason that the thought never occurred to me.' She then explained that she only attempted to justify herself when she was convinced that, on clinical grounds, I did not regard her as psychotic.

On April 26th she mentioned another of what she described as Roger's habits. 'He never ate or drank without saying the Lord's Prayer first!' The exclamation mark should be noted. She regarded Roger's prayer as one of his idiosyncrasies. She did not realise that this was the customary Cathar practice.[1]

[1] See René Nelli's *La vie Quotidienne des Cathares de Languedoc au XIII^{ieme} siécle* (Hachette. Paris 1969).

35

I am not sure of the date of the following letter. 'I am very grateful indeed to have your reassurance that you believe me no matter what others may or may not say.' (She had not discussed her case with others. She is referring to the possibility of my being visited by a Professor from Toulouse. This gentleman was neither Professor Nelli nor Duvernoy but was recommended by the former to visit me if he could find the time to do so.) She wondered how I would react if the Professor decided that her far memory was spurious.) I replied that by opinion would not change. The question did not arise as the Professor, who was visiting London, failed to find time to visit me. Mrs. Smith, as an expression of her gratitude, wrote as follows. 'If, therefore, there is anything you want to know about Cathar ritual, I'll tell you. They weren't as peculiar as a good many historians make out. I'll tell you something.'

When she was excommunicated from the Roman Church she was required to undergo an acceptance ceremony into the Anglican community before she could be married in Church. Her description is as follows. 'He,' (the vicar) 'placed an open Bible over my head and said a lot of stuff which I can't remember. Then I had to make a complete denial of the Roman Church while he washed his hands and then I had to wash mine. This was very similar to the Cathar Convenanza, except that the latter took place in a house, and the whole congregation washed their hands. The active participants agreed to honour the priests and keep the fasts, but the rest of the service was practically the same right down to the denial of the Roman Church. Oh yes, and a lot of kissing always took place afterwards, but there's nothing too peculiar about that either when I think of the last Quaker meeting I attended.'

Mrs. Smith refers to the Convenanza. This was the promise made by the *croyant* to receive the Consolamentum at the hour of death. He renewed this promise every time he greeted a Parfait in case he should be unable to speak at the time of death. The promise made by the *croyant* was morally binding upon the Parfaits. They must, if it were at all physically possible, give him the Consolamentum on his death bed. Having made the pact of the Convenanza the *croyant* could still receive the Consolamentum on his deathbed even though he was so ill that he had lost the power of speech. (As we will see later, this question of the Convenanza, the Consolamentum and the ability to speak, is of cardinal importance in assessing the date of Roger's death.)

Now what I have said of the Convenanza is a summary of the views of the experts. Mrs. Smith questions their conclusions. In a letter of May 16th, 1969, she said, in discussing the above orthodox definition of the Convenanza, 'I don't altogether go along with that! I believe that the Convenanza was an agreement/pact made before entry into the Cathar faith, containing *one* promise alone—that was to be ready always to be at the disposal of the Parfaits, if needed, and to honour them.

'Maybe later on when the Inquisitors wrongly charged them with forcing the last rites of the Cathar Church upon the dying when they didn't desire it, they decided to include as part of the Convenanza the Consolamentum on the death bed, but this promise wasn't there originally and I feel it wasn't strictly necessary. After all, taking Roman Catholics for instance, they don't go in for special agreements concerning the Last Rites at the hour of death—they automatically expect as members of the Church that it will be administered to them when the time comes. I really am sorry to confuse the issue by disagreeing with the experts. I make no claim to be right, although it would take a lot more than these experts to persuade me that I am wrong! I feel that the Cathar doctrines were obviously not accurately recorded at the time. One reads it up in Guiraud etc. and it all sounds rather fussy, strict and complicated, but of course it wasn't. I repeat, as I have always done, that the Cathar faith was simple and the idea that their beliefs and practices were unnatural and immoral is quite untrue.'

The above makes very good sense. It is quite easy to picture the Catholics making allegations that the moribund were forced to take the Consolamentum on their death beds. After all they have alleged much worse against the Cathars. Mrs. Smith's idea that the earlier form of the Convenanza was amended in order to rebut these libels seems altogether reasonable.

Another point in favour of Mrs. Smith's contention is that it stresses the obligation of the *croyant* to be at the disposal of the Parfait. Now our sources of information, Roman Catholic and otherwise, stress that the *croyant* was expected to 'adore' that is to say to genuflect before the Parfait. Naturally the Roman Catholic sources accentuate the malign influence of this act. But there is little written evidence that the *croyants* were expected to show implicit obedience to their priests. Now unquestioning and self-sacrificing obedience towards his priest was required of the simple believer in the early form of Dualism practised by Manes. The detractors of the Manichæens have emphasised this point with relish. It is possible that a simple promise of obedience to the priest was the original form of the Convenanza and that in this the Cathars were following the tradition of their Manichæen predecessors. After all nobody questions that Catharism, if it does not have its origin in Manichæen dualism, presents considerable similarities to the latter faith.

Here again it is a question of Mrs. Smith against the standard authorities. Once more we must wait for the appearance of further evidence, though it is perhaps too much to hope for this happy occurrence after the lapse of seven centuries. But a person who, in her far memory, has been so right about so many things, may well be correct in this her latest contention. One thing, too, should be remembered whenever we speak of her as in conflict with the standard authorities. By the latter term one means those who have reigned in the past. In modern times there are none more qualified to speak than Professor Nelli and Monsieur Duvernoy, both of whom on more than one occasion corrected errors in previous so-called standard works. Both these distinguished men have treated with the greatest respect the

146

evidence produced, through my agency, by Mrs. Smith.

'I'm pretty certain the Cathar services were in the vernacular and *not* in Latin.' She is absolutely right. The fact that the services were mostly in Occitan was a crime in the eyes of the Papacy. 'They, the Cathars, went in for a lot of repetition of the same prayer, saying it several times straight off.' Once again Mrs. Smith is correct. The constant repetition of prayers, and particularly the Lord's Prayer, is recorded by many historians as a Cathar habit.[2]

In a letter dated July 11th she said, 'I could tell you a lot more about Roger, but I'm not deliberately trying to hold things back from you. It's just that I'm so stupidly shy that I can't say them.' She made it quite clear that her shyness was not related to her physical love for him. It was obvious that her feeling for Roger was still very precious to her.

She then went on to talk about meditation. She said, 'It is simply a way of finding peace with a receptive mind open to Divine influence, so that one acquires the power of spiritual perception. In brief, an awareness of the presence of Christ.'

I regret that I have not space in this book to write more about Mrs. Smith's ideas about life and in particular her religious ideas. It would provide a suitable background to her former life as a Cathar and would reveal perhaps what she learnt from it. It is worth while quoting from a letter dated July 21st 1967. I had raised at some time or other the question of meditation, probably in relation to Catharism. I was very positively interested as to whether they practised any particular form of meditation. She wrote, 'Do you see it as a remedy for the stress and strain of life? I wonder if it is wise to aim too high or make a conscious effort to enter a new dimension of spiritual life. Are the English, as a race, intelligent enough to discriminate between true enlightenment and the psuedo-spiritual? I used to meditate when I was a young girl, but never consciously, for perhaps all I ever wanted was to find peace. One cannot find peace if one's mind is fluttering about like a trapped bird, and when I'm in this state

[2] See René Nelli's *La Vie Quotidienne des Cathares* Hachette. Paris 1969.

a relaxed, effortless concentration is impossible. Peace comes to me from time to time. I desire it—we all do—but I don't make an all-out effort to find it.'

36

One may now sum up how far one has got and what else one is looking for. One set out to find whether Fabrissa was an individual and, if so, whether she was related to a veritable historical character called Pierre de Mazerolles. These facts are established beyond doubt. So are those concerning Fabrissa's immediate friends and relations, including Roger. A fuller dossier of these characters will be produced in the next section. The lesser characters such as Mir de Camplong and the second Roger will also be identified more fully, though we know already of the former that he was a gentleman of strong Cathar leanings with estates in the Corbières, who was a friend of Roger's and present at the siege of Fanjeaux. We have still some way to go in identifying the second Roger.

One would have thought that to identify the above across the gulf of seven centuries would be satisfying enough but Mrs. Smith, in spite of the way history coincided with her revelations, was still mistrustful of her own evidence. On February 3rd, 1967, she was still saying that, if Roger had beyond any doubt a sister called Helis and if she had married into the Mazerolles family, this would provide what she called the missing link. She was even more concerned to be reassured that Arnaud de Mazerolles was Helis' husband. Fortunately at this time I received letters and family trees from Monsieur Duvernoy and Professor Nelli which placed the matter beyond all doubt.

Her hesitation was attributable to that part of her nature which did not want her to believe. She had never gloried in her psychic potentialities and wished herself without them. Secondly, she was scrupulously truthful. Thirdly, I feel, though I say this with caution, that she was over-troubled by the description de

148

Grisolles. The fact that Roger is not mentioned in the records by this designation bothered her considerably. I have already spoken of my leap into the dark in saying that his name was given to him because of his poetic tendencies. Another possibility arises. In recording her revelations, she may have found difficulty in picking up the word Isarn and Grisolles may be the nearest guess. Admittedly this is a long shot but we are, after all, dealing with a girl of thirteen taking down phonetically, possibly in a state of clair-audience, information in a foreign language, in its mediaeval form and, very important, almost certainly spoken in a throaty accent. Ordinary French, as distinct from Occitan and the local patois, is, to this day, hard enough for the visitor to the Languedoc to comprehend.

In an accompanying letter Mrs. Smith emphasised that Roger and Alaïs were of noble birth. 'At that time they certainly lived in a large house near Montbrun.' This all fits in. Montbrun in the Aude, is in a neighbourhood where the nobility were almost exclusively Cathar.[1] The Fanjeaux, Durfort (Feste) and de Mazerolles families all lived in this locality. She said, 'The de Mazerolles must have been a wealthy lot, too. Fabrissa had her own place which looked like a small castle.' This is absolutely in keeping with the description in the Inquisitorial records of Fabrissa acting as a hostess in her own right to heretics. Mrs. Smith continues to say of Fabrissa's house, 'It seemed always to be crowded, and sometimes the meetings were held there'. This means that Fabrissa, following a common procedure, became a Parfaite after years of marriage and ran a large house separate from that of her husband.

By the first months of 1967 I had narrowed down the scene of the drama to the cluster of towns constituted by Fanjeaux, Montréal, Laurac and Mazerolles, each not more than seven or eight kilometres from each other, and to the wild hills of the Corbières lying East and South. I was satisfied that this area

[1] Mrs. Smith herself says this Montbrun where Roger and Helis lived was quite different from the one near Foix. Her memories of Roger preaching in the latter are especially vivid.

was the stage for the activities of the families in which we are chiefly interested, i.e. those of Fanjeaux, Mazerolles and Laurac. I have already described how I found my way to the Durfort house at Fanjeaux, the home of Guillaume the troubadour and grandfather of Roger. My discovery in 1966 of the Durfort castle deep in the country was still more what, had it been an isolated occurrence could have been called fortuitous, but which, against the background of what had been said, was again directed.

My wife and I were driving along a lonely road in the departement of Aude when I saw an inconspicuous signpost to the chateau of Durfort. There was no way to the ruins except through the private grounds of a country house. I felt diffident about walking down the avenue without permission. I then saw a woman and man coming towards me. I asked if it was possible to look at the ruins. The man said that the property was private but that he was sure it would be alright but in any case the owner was at hand. He pointed out the latter, who was digging in the garden and who willingly gave us permission to go and look at the ruins. We had not set off with any intention of looking for the Chateau de Durfort. I did not know that there was any Durfort property in existence other than the house at Fanjeaux.

I had not realised until early in 1967 how much our principal characters played their part on a relatively circumscribed stage. Certainly Roger travelled considerably but the main possessions of his family, and of those to whom they were related and friendly, were concentrated in a limited area. For instance, the distance between Fanjeaux and Dufort is less than thirty English miles. These facts make Mrs. Smith's story all the more credible.

A further point as to the scene of our history. Professor Nelli wrote to inform me that St. Papoul and St. Paul de Jarratt, with which Mrs. Smith was so preoccupied, were both very active centres of heresy.

37

It now remains to complete and assess the historical evidence for Mrs. Smith's story. This involves three tasks, the full identification of the main characters, of the regions which they inhabited and the period in which they lived.

Our main characters are Roger, Helis, Fabrissa and Pierre de Mazerolles. These names constantly appear in Mrs. Smith's dreams, visions and memories. What is the evidence of their existence? The latter is proved beyond doubt by study of the records and consultation of authorities on the subject. The main book references are Guiraud's *Histoire de l'Inquisition au Moyen Age*. Much of his information is extracted from the Doat Collection in the Bibliothèque National in Paris. Perhaps the most useful writings of all, though less voluminous than Guiraud, are those of Jean Duvernoy, who has gone into the question of the heretical families of the Lauragais with great care and devotion. Other book references are mentioned in the index.

As well as studying the written evidence I have received immense help from René Nelli, Professor of Literature at Toulouse, and from Monsieur Duvernoy. Both are aware that my sources of information are highly unusual. Both have taken what I have said with great seriousness. The more I have told them the more aid they have offered. In the first letter he wrote to me Monsieur Duvernoy expressed admiration for my detailed knowledge of Catharism. All this was acquired in confirming the truth of Mrs. Smith's experiences. Professor Nelli has on more than one occasion expressed his astonishment at her revelations and advised me that when in doubt one should go by what she says. Both Professor Nelli and Monsieur Duvernoy have answered numerous specific questions addressed by me to them and arising out of Mrs. Smith's far memories. On all the main issues they have confirmed what she said. In one or two less important issues confirmatory evidence has not been available.

In the case of the Parfait Imbert, Monsieur Duvernoy says that his fate is unknown and Mrs. Smith that he died at the stake. Over an issue like this one cannot take sides. I would, however, bet heavily that if the appropriate information comes to light about Imbert (Raimond Imbert of Moissac) it will be found that he suffered as Mrs. Smith indicates.

I cannot recall any issue of any importance where Mrs. Smith's memory is proved false by reliable historical evidence. Certainly she described Imbert as a Bishop rather than a Parfait—had he been a Bishop he would still have been a Parfait—but to expect hundred per cent accuracy in such an issue is surely pedantic and in any case Imbert is only a minor character in her story and, in addition, known to few enough students of Catharism.

The biggest issue on which she is at odds with the historians is the date of Roger's death. This cannot be used against her. There is nothing in the records to give us the exact date. As we shall see later, the approximate date recorded in Helis' deposition just does not fit the other available facts.

Mrs. Smith has always asserted that Alaïs (Helis) de Mazerolles was Roger's sister, that both were members of the Fanjeaux family, that Helis married Arnaud de Mazerolles, and that Roger remained unmarried. This is absolutely true according to the evidence supplied by Guiraud, The Doat Collection, Monsieur Duvernoy, Professor Nelli and others. It is also revealed in Helis' testimony before the Inquisition on August 5th, 1243.

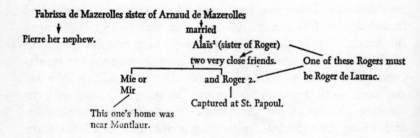

Fabrissa de Mazerolles sister of Arnaud de Mazerolles

↓   ↓
Pierre her nephew.   married

                                         Alaïs[1] (sister of Roger) ⟍
                                         two very close friends.   One of these Rogers must
                              ⌐   ⌐   be Roger de Laurac.
                              Mie or   and Roger 2. ⟋
                              Mir |
                                                 Captured at St. Papoul.
                         This one's home was
                         near Montlaur.

[1] Otherwise Helis.

This is a family tree produced by Mrs. Smith long before I obtained the genealogical evidence from Professor Nelli and Monsieur Duvernoy, from the depositions made by Helis de Mazerolles and others before the Inquisition, and from a careful study of Guiraud's classic. I set it out in the exact form in which Mrs. Smith supplied it.

The historical records previously mentioned show that the Fanjeaux family consisted of the following: —

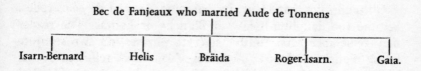

Bec de Fanjeaux who married Aude de Tonnens

Isarn-Bernard   Helis   Bräida   Roger-Isarn.   Gaia.

The same sources show that Fabrissa de Mazerolles was the sister-in-law of Helis and Roger. The unfortunate Helis was the mother of the blackguardly Pierre de Mazerolles. The saintly Fabrissa was the latter's aunt. Roger-Isarn was our Roger.

38

HELIS DE MAZEROLLES.

Let us consider first the case of Helis because more is known of her than any other member of the Fanjeaux family. She is first recorded in 1198 at the house in Fanjeaux of Guillelme de Tonnens.[1] This house was placed openly at the disposition of the heretics. Helis is described as the daughter of Aude and as having later become a Parfaite. On this particular visit little Helis received only wine, bread, nuts and fruit as refreshment. Guillelme was obviously practising the austerities necessary in a Parfaite. Later Guiraud says that Bräida (see family tree) was

[1] Guiraud, *Histoire d'Inquisition.* Vol. 1 page 289, and also in her deposition before the Inquisition (Doat Collection).

the sister of a 'zealous believer', Helis de Mazerolles.[2] Professor Nelli states that Helis was the grand-daughter of the troubadour Guillaume de Durfort. This relationship becomes more important when we are discussing the identity of her brother Roger. Oth de Niort, a heretical nobleman and a determined opponent of Catholicism, remembered as a child seeing Helis about 1206 at the House of Blanche de Laurac. Mir de Camplong and Roger de la Tour were also present. The two latter are the two friends of Puerilia's Roger.

Guiraud says that Helis, in marrying Arnaud de Mazerolles, became the daughter-in-law of Blanche de Laurac. The reader may remember Mrs. Smith's staccato phrases, on two separate lines, 'Blanche de Laurac' and 'Roger's mother', followed by the statement that this must not be taken to indicate inevitably that Blanche was Roger's mother. She was in fact the mother-in-law of the principal Roger, i.e. Roger-Isarn, in our story. It is, however, possible that in the second of these brief phrases Mrs. Smith is referring to the second Roger, who bore the surname of de la Tour de Laurac.

Elsewhere Guiraud[3] describes Helis as related to all the nobility of Montréal, Gaja, Laurac and Fanjeaux. He describes how she was concerned with the finances of the Cathar cause. This is an extract of major importance. Firstly he categorically describes Pierre as her son. Secondly, he makes clear Pierre's interest in money, a point abundantly stressed by Mrs. Smith (we shall deal with this later when discussing Pierre.) Helis is also described as hearing Bertrand Marty, the Parfait, preach in a field near Gaja. This was in 1237. On this occasion she was accompanied by her son Pierre. She heard the same preacher in 1239 but this time in the company of Fabrissa de Mazerolles[4] and Pons de Capelli.

The most important evidence of all is that of Helis herself. It is fascinating that we should be able to locate the very date on

[2] *Histoire d'Inquisition.* Vol. 1. page 270.
[3] Jean Guiraud. *Histoire d'Inquisition au Moyen Age.* Vol. 1. Page 353.
[4] Jean Duvernoy. Bertrand Marty. *Cahiers d'Etudes Cathares.* Autumn 1968.

which the Inquisitors interrogated this woman, whose name first came to us, across the centuries, on a scrap of paper written by Mrs. Smith when doing her ironing in a West Country village. The date in question was August 5th, 1243. She is described[5] unequivocally as the former wife of Arnaud de Mazerolles. In her deposition she admits that, round about 1195, she was present with several others at religious meetings at which the famous Cathar Bishop Guilbert de Castres was present. She also refers, in the course of interrogation, to her visit to Guillelme de Tonnens which we have previously mentioned. She describes Fabrissa de Mazerolles as her sister-in-law and says that the latter directed a house for heretics at Montréal. Among people mentioned as having been present at heretical gatherings held there in 1210 were Aimeric de Montréal (son of Blanche de Laurac) and the three brothers Pierre, Arnaud and Raines de Mazerolles. This was round about 1210. She mentions the same people as having been present at another meeting and in another house five years previously.

Helis testified that in 1210 she had also seen Fabrissa at Gaja in heretical company which included Mir de Camplong and Arnaud de Mazerolles. She also described how in 1210 Fabrissa took part in a Cathar ceremony called the *apparellhamentum*. This was a kind of monthly prayer meeting with a set form of public confession.

It is clear from her testimony that her sister Gaia shared the faith of her family. She is described as taking part in heretical activities round about 1228. There are further references to other members of her family , e.g. Veziada, wife of her brother Isarn-Bernard. Both husband and wife were later sentenced to life imprisonment.

References to Pierre and Arnaud de Mazerolles continue in Helis' testimony. She describes them as being engaged in heretical activities as late as 1240. Mir de Camplong is mentioned as similarly occupied in 1238.

From the point of view of our study the most important item

[5] Doat Collection. Folio 162. Bibliotheque National Paris.

in her testimony is her reference to her brother Roger-Isarn. This can, however, be more logically dealt with in the section devoted to the establishment of his identity.

The evidence quoted confirms completely the existence, the identity and the relationships of Helis de Mazerolles as described by Mrs. Smith.

One point of special interest arises. In the first sentence of the deposition Helis is described as the *former* wife of Arnaud de Mazerolles. The obvious explanation is that she became a Parfaite by mutual consent of her husband. Many Parfaites were recruited in this way. It is just possible that there may be another explanation and that her relationship with her husband may not have been completely harmonious. On one occasion Puerilia asked Helis 'why did you marry him?' After an interval of more than seven centuries this is a point which cannot be elucidated. It shows, however, that in some particulars Mrs. Smith can perhaps tell us more about Helis than the Inquisitors.

39

FABRISSA DE MAZEROLLES.

Enough has been said in the note about Helis to establish Fabrissa's identity as the sister-in-law of Helis and Roger and the aunt of Pierre. A good deal of our information about Fabrissa is derived from Helis' deposition. Here are a few additional notes. Guiraud says that she belonged to one of the most noble families of the neighbourhood,[1] and that in 1209 she lent her house for Cathar meetings.

In 1233 or 1234 the Cathar Bishop Guilbert de Castres preached and received the respectful genuflexions (called by the Cathars adoration) of Fabrissa and Raines de Mazerolles as well as Roger's friend Mir de Camplong. This event took place in the

[1] *Histoire d'Inquisition au Moyen Age.* Vol. 1. page 270.

house of Pons de Villeneuve. Fabrissa, before becoming a Parfaite, was married to Bernard de Villeneuve.[2]

Zoë Oldenbourg in the *Massacre at Montségur* also refers to Fabrissa as an active protector of heretics.

Professor Nelli of Carcassonne in a letter to me described her as the sister-in-law of Helis, the aunt of Pierre de Mazerolles and the wife of Bernard de Villeneuve. He also indicated that before writing to me he had studied the notes made by his deceased friend Adibert of Montréal, who had compiled a file devoted to Fabrissa.

Again the existence and identity of Fabrissa cannot be doubted. That she was a person of importance is equally clear. She is described as being the head of one of the Cathar houses which had some resemblance to convents. This gives substance to one of the key statements of Mrs. Smith's story. 'If you get into trouble go to Fabrissa.' Professor Nelli, in commenting on Mrs. Smith's description of life in the institution for women, says categorically that this must have been the house directed by Fabrissa at Montréal.

40

PIERRE DE MAZEROLLES.

The references to this man are numerous. We have encountered several already in our notes on Helis and Fabrissa. He is described by Guiraud[1] as one of three brothers who were among the most active antagonists of Catholicism. On page 353 Volume I the author refers to him categorically as the son of Helis. He states that the latter was concerned in the financial affairs of the Cathars and implies that her son Pierre's interest in finance was less orthodox and that he used his mother's influence with the Cathars to procure money from them. About 1232 he borrowed

[2] *Histoire d'Inquisition au Moyen Age.* Vol. 2. page 84.
[1] *Histoire d'Inquisition au Moyen Age.* Vol. 1. p. 290.

money from the Parfait Bertrand Marty in exchange for a promise of safe conduct. Such practices were usual in the Languedoc at that time but, as well as Mrs. Smith's estimate of his character, we have other evidence of his greed, as we shall see later in studying the affair at Avignonet. It is recorded that in 1232 the Parfait Bertrand Marty was living in the Selve and was in contact, among others, with Pierre de Mazerolles.[2] In the same year he was present in the escort which accompanied Guilhabert de Castres and other Parfaits when they met Raimon de Pereille.[3] In 1237 Marty preached in a field at Gaja for Helis de Mazerolles and Pierre.[4] He is also mentioned in Zoë Oldenbourg's book as one of the seven men who claimed to have inflicted mortal wounds on the two Inquisitors.

Our knowledge of the part played by Pierre de Mazerolles in the massacre of the Inquisitors is quite considerable. Because his rôle at Avignonet coincides so closely with his character as revealed by Mrs. Smith it is important to describe this affair in some detail.

The two Inquisitors, Guillaume Arnaud and Pierre Seila, had been very active and very efficient in the Languedoc in the early twelve forties. The tension mounted steeply towards Ascension day in 1242. Our story moves also to its climax. The two Inquisitors took the road via Castelnaudary to Avignonet. There they were received cordially and treacherously by Raymond d'Alfar who offered them hospitality in the name of the Count of Toulouse, whose agent he was.[5] Note well that the name Alfar occurs in Mrs. Smith's memories. D'Alfar then met two knights, Guillaume de la Plaigne and Jordanet du Mas at the forest of Antioch near Mas-Saint Puelles. D'Alfar informed de la Plaigne that the Count of Toulouse had been unable to contact either Pierre de Mazerolles or the other gentry who wished to kill the Inquisitors and their companions. The motive for their liquidation was, of course, the protection of the heavily heretical

[2] Jean Duvernoy. *Bertrand Marty. Cahiers d'Etudes Cathares.* Autumn 1968.
[3] René Nelli *La Vie Quotidienne des Cathares.*
[4] Guiraud. *Histoire d'Inquisition* Vol. 2. page 82.
[5] Guiraud. *Inquisition au Moyen Age.* Vol. 2. page 118.

families, whose names appeared in the records of the ever active and watchful Inquisition. It is obvious that de la Plaigne made contact with Pierre de Mazerolles because the latter appeared quickly enough on the scene.

In addition, d'Alfar also gave a letter to de la Plaigne to transmit to Pierre-Roger de Mirepoix, Commander of the garrison at Montségur. The latter was asked to bring a troop of knights and soldiers to Avignonet. D'Alfar undertook to hand over the Inquisitors to Pierre Roger and his men. It is obvious that he also arranged for Pierre Roger to meet Pierre de Mazerolles because this is what subsequently happened. In his journey from Montségur Pierre Roger de Mirepoix stopped in a wood near Gaja. Note again that this was the centre of the Mazerolles possessions. A short time afterwards Pierre de Mazerolles arrived. He had an interview with Pierre-Roger de Mirepoix, following which he left him to return with Jourdain du Villas, Pierre Viel and twenty-five men of Gaja furnished with axes and other weapons. As the tension rises it is fascinating to reflect that what was to follow should reverberate in the dreams of a girl in the West of England seven centuries and more later.

The conjoined force then split up in order to avoid attention. Twelve sergeants at arms were chosen from among the twenty-five who accompanied Pierre de Mazerolles. These twelve, armed with axes and led by Bernard de Saint-Martin, set off for Avignonet and were admitted to the house where the Inquisitors were lodged. The latter and their entourage were killed without delay. Guiraud gives the names of those who actually struck the fatal blows or who claimed to have done so. This does not correspond to the same list supplied by Zoë Oldenbourg though the name of Pierre Vidal[6] is common to both. But Pierre de Mazerolles is definitely cited by Zoë Oldenbourg as having boasted that he had inflicted mortal wounds on the Inquisitors.

It is at this stage that Mrs. Smith's account reflects her uncanny accuracy in these matters. It will be remembered how in her dream Pierre de Mazerolles returns in a state of macabre

[6] *No relation to the famous troubadour.*

exhilaration. She described him as elated and happy at having killed. According to the deposition of Imbert de Salas the same air of sinister exuberance coloured the whole proceedings. When Pierre-Roger de Mirepoix saw G. Acermat, one of the executioners of the Inquisitors, he cried 'Traitor, where is then the cup of Arnaud?' The latter was one of the dead inquisitors. Cup was Pierre-Roger's jocular rendering of skull.

Acermat replied, 'It is broken'.

'And why haven't you brought back the fragments?' Pierre-Roger continued, 'I would have joined them together with a band of gold and drunk wine out of this cup all my life.'[7] Pierre de Mazerolles was still fevered by this blood curdling hilarity when he went into the room where Mrs. Smith was sleeping. Its echoes persisted till five years ago.

Mrs. Smith described Pierre de Mazerolles as no true Cathar but instigated only by greed. In this connection it is fascinating to contemplate the behaviour of the Knights at Avignonet after the murder. Zoë Oldenbourg comments as follows on the scene which preceded the massacre. 'Then the booty was shared; the registers of the Inquisitors, the few objects of value they carried with them in their journeyings; little enough, books, a candle stick, a box of ginger, some silver coins, clothes, blankets (couvertures), scapulaires, knives. To see the greed with which these men who, without being rich, were by no means poor, hurled themselves on objects which were, after all, of little value, in a room strewn with disfigured and bleeding corpses, gives the impression of a distribution of trophies rather than a scene of pillage. Those of the conspirators who had not participated in the murder joined with the others, each wishing to have his portion.'

This description of infantile greed plus nervous exaltation in killing, though admittedly applied to a whole group of men, symbolises beautifully Mrs. Smith's description of Pierre de Mazerolles. We have referred elsewhere to this preoccupation with money in the matter of Bertrand Marty and to the way he

[7] Zoë Oldenbourg. *The Massacre at Montségur.*

profited with his mother's position in the Cathar community to strike bargains for himself.

Guiraud on page 123 of Volume 2, goes on to say that Pierre-Roger de Mirepoix 'had been haunted, in the course of this tragic night, by the desire to have news of the Count of Toulouse'. This means that he wished to know what support he could expect, against the inevitable Catholic reaction following the murder of the Inquisitors, from the vacillating and unpredictable Raymond of Toulouse who combined tolerance of heretics with a desire to placate the Papacy and the Kingdom of France in order to preserve his possessions. Before setting off on his return to Montségur Pierre-Roger sent two Sergeants at Arms to Isarn de Fanjeaux to find out what attitude the Count was taking. Isarn de Fanjeaux was Roger's brother. I do not think it possible that this was the Roger-Isarn in which we are interested. Firstly, our central character must have been known as Roger in the family and his elder brother as Isarn. How otherwise could their friends and relatives have distinguished between Isarn-Bernard and Roger-Isarn? Secondly, Puerilia always referred to her friend as Roger. Thirdly, Isarn appears more frequently in the historical records than Roger and was obviously more active in public life, as he must well have been in order to be in the confidence of the Count of Toulouse. Fourthly, Mrs. Smith's description of Roger is not that of a man engaged in affairs of state. He was essentially a gentle, reflective soul, a serious minded Cathar much given to reflection on the sinfulness of the world and not prone to any kind of violence.

What this extract from Guiraud does confirm is the importance of the Fanjeaux family in the Cathar fraternity.[8] More interesting

---

[8] I have recently acquired more positive evidence of this. On October 3rd, 1969 Monsieur Jean Duvernoy provided me with a still more comprehensive family tree than that which he had sent me before. This shows that Helis and Roger were cousins of Pierre Roger de Mirepoix the elder, that is to say of the father of the commander of the garrison at Montségur. This close family relationship, as well as the fact that the individuals concerned had estates in close proximity to each other, explains how Mrs. Smith was able to remember so many of the pillars and props of Catharism in the Lauragais and the Corbières.

to us is the point that, even though Pierre-Roger de Mirepoix made contact with Roger's brother as soon as possible, it is likely that our own Roger knew as early or earlier than his brother. It was surely with this object in view that Pierre de Mazerolles burst into the room in which Puerilia was sleeping. That he tried to kiss her may well have been a by-product of his morbid exaltation.

Enough has been said to show that what history knows of Pierre de Mazerolles confirms remarkably Mrs. Smith's experience of him. This is all the more satisfying because in starting one's researches he was the only character of which one possessed the full name.

I had always assumed that nothing further was known of the activities of Pierre de Mazerolles following the affair at Avignonet. Certainly he does not seem to have been immediately apprehended for his part in the massacre. I had thought it possible that he ended his life as a *faidit*, the name given to dispossessed knights who lived as outlaws and maintained a clandestine opposition to the occupying powers. But I learned from Monsieur Duvernoy in October 1969 that he appeared before the Inquisition on July 12th, 1246, that is to say four years after the massacre at Avignonet.[9] His capacity for survival appears to have been considerable. There is no record of his having received any sentence. This is not to say that he escaped unpunished but he appears to have had a considerable gift for extricating himself from difficult situations. Why he did not appear before the Inquisition till 1246 is very strange. Of course we must remember Mrs. Smith's assessment of his character. He had no real concern for Catharism and his only love was money. He may well have either done a deal with the occupying powers or affected collaboration with them. In any case all we know about him accords well with Mrs. Smith's description of his character.

[9] Manuscript No. 609 de la Bibliotheque de Toulouse.

41

ROGER-ISARN.

We will now consider what, to Mrs. Smith at any rate, was the central figure of the story. We know for certain his immediate connections. We have the names of his three sisters, Helis, Bräida and Gaia and of his brother, Isarn-Bernard. Helis also spoke of him as her brother in her disposition. In actual fact less is known of him than of his brother and of his sisters, Helis and Braïda.[1] He and Gaia obtrude less in history than the other members of the family. We know that Isarn-Bernard was condemned to life imprisonment and that Helis was interrogated by the Inquisition. For our main facts about Roger we have to rely on Mrs. Smith.

There are two positive references to Roger-Isarn. By far the most important is that made by Helis in her deposition of August 5th, 1243. This is of fascinating interest not because it proves clearly for us the existence of Roger and that he was Helis' brother but because its whole import is mysterious. Helis referred to Roger as her former brother. He must therefore, unless Helis was giving false evidence, have died before 1243 or earlier than August of that year. She describes him as having been taken ill in the house of Gaillard de Feste at Fanjeaux. De Feste was the name of the Durfort family to which Roger was related. The deposition says that he was stricken with the illness from which he died. The question is, does the Latin phrase *illa infirmitata qua obiit* mean that he died on the occasion of this illness or that at this time he was suffering from a malady from which he expired later at some unspecified date.

Now Helis says, when making her deposition, that this occurred eighteen years or more previously, that is to say round about 1225. In his annotation of the deposition,

[1] Braïda is known to have been a Parfaite.

made in a personal communication, Monsieur Duvernoy suggests 1227.

But Mrs. Smith insists that Roger lived until 1243. Certainly he was alive at the time of the massacre of the Inquisitors in 1242. It cannot be doubted that her main recurring dream involved the return of Pierre de Mazerolles from the massacre. She is equally certain that Roger expressed his horror and disgust at this crime. Are the Inquisitorial records inaccurate? They could well be. They are in certain places very vague. They seem to follow a stock formula. At this particular sitting of the Inquisition it seems that all that was required of the accused was that he or she admitted to having kept company with heretics and revealed as many names of his co-believers as possible. Each item in the deposition was followed by an obviously rough estimate of the time elapsed since the accused had seen his fellow malefactors.

Helis' deposition covers forty-two paragraphs, excluding the single line insertions devoted to the lapse of time since the incidents described. She goes right back to 1195. As this was forty-eight years before the date of her interrogation she is not incriminating any considerable number of people. A large proportion of those mentioned as having been heretics in 1195 must have been dead by 1243. Only three of her forty-two paragraphs deal with dates including and after 1240. One gets the impression she is giving little away. In contrast the testimony of Arnaud Roger de Mirepoix, contains a far higher proportion of later dates approachng that of his interrogation on April 22nd, 1244.

Was Helis hiding the date of Roger's death or was it merely that her statement was wrongly recorded? As I have said the records follow a set pattern. They give an impression of being a rough job, and were probably written in great haste by not very literate clerks at the dictation of Inquisitors tired by a hard day's persecution and not too obsessed by accuracy. One is not criticising the efficiency of their interrogators but merely suggesting that they were not over preoccupied with the keeping of the records.

164

All this is conjecture. There is, however, one point on which we can be certain. Roger could *not* have died on the occasion described by Helis.

The deposition says that he was so ill that he had lost the power of speech. The famous Bishop Guilbert de Castres was present. Nevertheless the Consolamentum was *not* administered. This is a vital point. It was laid down that the Consolamentum could only be administered to those in their right mind and fully conscious. Exception was made in the case of the dying. If Guilbert de Castres did not administer the Consolamentum to Roger it was because, in spite of the apparent seriousness of his condition, he knew that he was not dying.

There is another reference to the death of Roger. His brother, Isarn-Bernard, testified before the Inquisition that he had given the fifteen livres bequeathed to him by his brother to the Parfaits. Unfortunately no date of the death of his brother is specified.

We have to read the passage in Helis' deposition as indicating that when visited by Guilbert de Castres, Roger was suffering from the illness which *ultimately* caused his death. Have we any evidence from Mrs. Smith as to Roger's medical history? Yes, emphatically. Roger was very often ill, with a high fever. On one occasion he was thought to be dying. Mrs. Smith recalled in a letter written in 1966 the despair she felt on this occasion. Apart from this particular illness he often appeared exhausted and ill after his long journeys. He caught cold easily and was very susceptible to cold and damp.

It seems to me that Roger could well have been tubercular. His bouts of serious illness with high fever could have been pneumonia of tubercular origin.

One wonders why his tormentors threw cold water over him after other forms of torture had been applied. Perhaps he was ill already and they wished to expedite his end or perhaps they knew of his vulnerable point and hoped to provoke acute symptoms. Mrs. Smith insists that he died in prison of a chest infection. Now we know that Roger was incarcerated in a prison where male prisoners were allowed to be visited by their wives.

This means that he had not been formally condemned and that his case was being investigated. It is possible that, because Roger died under interrogation, whoever wrote up the case wished to insert a less incriminating reference to his death. It must be remembered that when sentence of death was passed the Inquisitors, unable themselves to shed blood, called in the secular arm for the execution of the sentence. Under these circumstances it was in the interests of the authorities to labour the fact that Roger had suffered on a previous occasion from an illness from which he died.

On August 31st, 1969, Mrs. Smith commented as follows on the preceding paragraphs of my manuscript. 'I'm sure you're absolutely right about Roger's illness being T.B. It would explain why he was so susceptible to the cold, the times when he came home completely exhausted, that persistent cough and the frequent bouts of feverishness. In Helis de Mazerolle's deposition she mentioned the illness from which her brother died. Did she, I wonder, put this bit in (and it does seem rather superfluous) to appease the Inquisitors? Were the latter sometimes rather touchy about their part in the murder of so many innocent victims? Far better to have Roger 'die of the illness from which he suffered for years' than to send him to the stake and arouse public sympathy. They treated him wickedly in prison; threw cold water over him, denied him anything to drink—aggravating his illness and bringing him to the speedy and desired end as effectively as the stake. Then technically they were good boys and not responsible for Roger's death. That would explain the ambiguity in Helis' deposition.'

In assessing the evidence given by Helis one must admit the more than possibility that it was extracted under torture and falsified to suit the requirements of the interrogators.

In his article on Bernard Marty in *Les Cahiers d'Etudes Cathares*, Monsieur Duvernoy mentions how, in 1225, the Parfait met, among other Knights, Roger-Isarn d'Arborens. This could possibly be an alternative name for Mrs. Smith's Roger. The meeting occurred at Laurac which is only a few miles from

Fanjeaux, the home of Roger's family. Even in thirteenth century Languedoc, where names were few, it is not likely that there was more than one Cathar member of the gentry in a very limited area bearing the name of Roger-Isarn. D'Arborens, like de Grisolles, could well have referred to another small estate possessed by Roger. It was the custom in these days and in that area for the nobility to possess quite small portions of land in several places.

So far then as official history is concerned we do not know the fate of Roger-Isarn. Is this surprising? He was, after all, a very minor character. The idea that Roger was moribund and did not receive the Consolamentum does not hold water. The description in the deposition is either a misstatement of fact or of interpretation. I am prepared to accept the advice expressed to me in a letter by Professor Nelli in which he indicated that when in doubt one should go by the patient.

Throughout this book, in expressing my opinions, I have been careful to lean on historical fact rather than on by own hunches. In this matter of the date of Roger's death I feel it necessary to be less rigid. Mrs. Smith has been proved right so often. Sometimes she has, as in the case of the colour of the Cathar priests' robes, been in advance of the savants. Her main recurring nightmare was obviously centred on the massacre of the Inquisitors. From what other murder could Pierre de Mazerolles be returning in a state of exaltation? She insists that Roger was alive at the time of the Avignonet affair. Her nightmare related to the latter stopped permanently following her first visit to me when she recognised me as Roger. The immediate cessation of this dream indicates the degree to which psychic communication was established. The far memory associated with this degree of communication is surely admissible as evidence, particularly as we have seen how often her recollections of the past conform strictly to the findings of history. And after all, in the case of Roger-Isarn, our chief historical source of information is the testimony of one woman, extracted under duress and possibly torture and, as I have argued, possibly wrongly recorded or

167

deliberately falsified. The whole pattern of Mrs. Smith's revelations point to Roger-Isarn being alive in or after 1242.

Finally, since writing the foregoing paragraphs, I have been told (October 3rd, 1969) by Monsieur Duvernoy in Toulouse, that in assessing dates mentioned in the depositions of Helis and others it is necessary to allow for a margin of error of twenty years. This is because the archives themselves are copies made two hundred years after the events they record. In making these copies errors of transcription have lead in places to an error of twenty years. If one accepts Monsieur Duvernoy's previous approximate date of Roger's death as 1227, allowing for an error of the above-mentioned dimensions, he would certainly be alive at the time of the massacre at Avignonet, which accords with Mrs. Smith's recollections.

42

ROGER'S FRIENDS. (THE OTHER ROGER AND MIR DE CAMPLONG.)

The second Roger is to be identified not merely by isolated references to him but because he is on several occasions described as being associated with Mir de Camplong. We have the clue from Mrs. Smith that these two were great friends of the first Roger. As the two Rogers went everywhere together, and as Mir was also a friend of the first Roger, any mention of him in the company of the second Roger is of significance. We are, after all, considering a small group of nobles in a restricted geographical area. Mir de Camplong is also referred to in the records as in the company of other members of the Laurac family.

Roger de la Tour and Mir de Camplong are described as being together at a Cathar meeting in 1209.[1] Both are referred to as coming from Laurac. This latter fact need not confuse us, because

[1] Guiraud. *Histoire d'Inquisition au Moyen Age.* Vol. 1. page 287.

of the Languedocien tradition of piecemeal estates in different areas. At one time the Mirepoix estate was divided among thirty-six owners.

Mir de Camplong and Fabrissa de Mazerolles are mentioned together by Guiraud.[2] This keeps Mir well within the circle of friends.

Mir de Camplong and Pons de la Tour are described as having taken part in heretical meetings at Laurac in 1223 and as being at that time *faidits*, that is to say out-lawed gentry. Monsieur Duvernoy also mentions how in the late Twelve-twenties Mir de Camplong was present when Guillaume Bernard de Laurac received the Consolamentum from Bertrand Marty.[3] Monsieur Duvernoy deals in this article with the incessant visits made to Montségur by the nobility of the Languedoc between 1236 and 1243. Among those mentioned are Pons de la Tour, described as the son of Roger de la Tour.

In 1233 Roger de la Tour, described by Guiraud as one of the Seigneurs of Laurac, received the Consolamentum from Bertrand Marty at the house of Bernard de Saint Martin.[4]

In 1237 the Inquisitors pronounced severe sentences against Isarn and Roger de la Tour de Laurac. (Was this following the second Roger being apprehended at St. Papoul, as Mrs. Smith remembered?) But then we learn that Roger de la Tour received the Consolamentum in 1238. It is quite inconceivable that, had he been undergoing a sentence of life imprisonment, he would have been permitted by the Catholics to receive a Parfait. It seems then that the severe sentences passed in 1237 did not involve death or life imprisonment. Possibly Isarn and Roger de la Tour were deprived of their property and received some sentence which left them at large. But certainly Mrs. Smith's second Roger also ended in prison.

One is helped as to the second Roger's identity by the knowledge of the first Roger's age. Roger was in his late fifties or

[2] Guiraud. *Histoire d'Inquisition au Moyen Age.* Vol. 2. page 84.
[3] Jean Duvernoy. *Cahiers d'Etudes Cathares.* Autumn 1968.
[4] Jean Duvernoy. *Cahiers d'Etudes Cathares.* Autumn 1968.

early sixties when he died. He was a great deal older than Puerilia. If one studies the references to Roger de la Tour and Mir de Camplong it is clear they were of the same generation. In the early years of my study of this subject I thought of Roger and his friends as much younger. Mrs. Smith did not inform me as to Roger's age until early in 1969. I certainly did not think of the second Roger as having had a family. This, as we have said previously, would not prevent him from becoming a Parfait at a later date. Herewith then, a further item of importance. At Toulouse, on August 11th, 1247, Pons de la Tour, described as a youth and as the son of Roger of the same name, was condemned to life imprisonment.[5]

The sentence was passed in the cloister of St. Sernin. This was where his father was also sentenced ten years previously. This throws some light on the reason why I persisted in doubting Mrs. Smith's preoccupation with St. Etienne. The Inquisition, as Molinier has pointed out, sat regularly in the cloister of the latter church. Nevertheless the second Roger and his son both suffered in the Church of St. Sernin. I suppose that, deep down in my unconscious, there was a recollection of this latter tragedy. My insistence that St. Sernin was the seat of the Inquisition was influenced by the fact that my friends had suffered there. Mrs. Smith, on the other hand, could only be positive about St. Etienne, where she herself had been held and from which she escaped.

One night in January 1969 the name Mir de Camplong kept breaking through my sleep. Just that, and the word diacre, and nothing more.

[5] Jean Guiraud. *Histoire d'Inquisition au Moyen Age*. Vol. 2. page 148.

43

OTHER MINOR CHARACTERS.
Blanche de Laurac.

It should be understood that minor, for the purpose of this book, means as far as Mrs. Smith's memories are concerned. For instance Blanche de Laurac appears several times in her schoolgirl notes. She is well known to any serious student of Catharism. She was known originally as Blanche de Montréal. She became a Parfaite after having borne nine children. One of these, Aimeric, assumed her title of de Montréal. This may have been after the death of his father or when his mother became a Parfaite. One of her sons was Arnaud, who married Helis. She is described by Guiraud as being in charge of several convents in the region of Laurac and Montréal. He says that the nobility of the region met regularly in her house. All these are obvious reasons why she should play a part in Mrs. Smith's recollections. Two of her children came to violent ends at the hands of the Crusaders. Aimeric was hanged and Guiraude, dame of Lavour, was thrown down a well and stones heaped upon her.

Bräida de Laurac.

Mrs. Smith's cryptic statement in two lines

Bräida de Laurac
Roger's mother.'

remains unexplained. She has always insisted that this is not to be taken as meaning that Bräida de Laurac was the mother of her own Roger. She wonders, and makes it clear that this is conjecture 'if Blanche de Laurac had a sister or sister-in-law named Bräida who with a bit of luck might have had a son Roger de la Tour de Laurac.' I throw out this hazard in the midst of so much certainty in the hope that some more competent authority than myself can answer the question.

Sicard and Guiraud d'Adalo.

It may be remembered that the above were sons of the old man G. d'Adalo who died at the siege of Fanjeaux so graphically described by Mrs. Smith. She indicated in one of her letters that they must have been soldiers because they were always fighting. They are referred to in the deposition made by Arnaud-Roger de Mirepoix before the Inquisition on April 22nd, 1244. They are specifically described as *chevaliers* (knights), which, in the Middle Ages, implied the right and the responsibility of carrying arms. After the name of their brother Gaucerand the word *miles* also appears. This is a more generic name for soldier. *Chevalier* more specifically designated the officer class.

What was the scene of the action of our drama? It is contained in the region known as the Lauragais. If you take a map of the department of the Aude and make a rough and tilted rectangle by drawing lines joining up Castelnaudary, Carcassonne, Limoux and Mirepoix you will be covering the main sites. Included within this area are Fanjeaux, Montréal, Mazerolles, and Laurac. The whole area is about thirty kilometres from west to east and rather less from north to south.

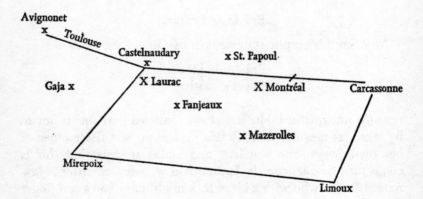

It contains, and adjoins, the place names constantly repeated in this story. Within the rectangle are Fanjeaux, Roger's native town, Laurac the home of his friend Roger, Mazerolles which belonged to the family of the same name and where Fabrissa gave shelter to heretics, and Montréal where she was the head of one of those Cathar houses for women which had some resemblance to convents. Fanjeaux and Montréal were both besieged and the site of terrible combats. Mrs. Smith has given us a graphic description of the siege of Fanjeaux.

Gaja, the principal possession of the de Mazerolles family, is a couple of kilometres west of the line Castelnaudary-Mirepoix.

St. Papoul, where the two Rogers were captured is, as the crow flies, about four miles north of the road from Castelnaudary to Carcassonne.

Avignonet, the scene of the massacre of the Inquisitors, lies west and slightly north of Castelnaudary. It is fourteen or fifteen miles distant from the latter place.

The very fact that so much of the action takes place within this limited area is further evidence of the truth of Mrs. Smith's story. In this small area were gathered together the families she knew and with which she consorted. The fact that the heretical families of Fanjeaux, de Mazerolles, Laurac and de Feste were so active in this region must also influence us in our attitude to other places mentioned by Mrs. Smith. For instance Montbrun and Montgaillard come into this story. Now there are places with these names in and around the Eastern Pyrenees, the former less than thirty kilometres east of Carcassonne and the latter a slightly greater distance to the south east of that city. At the same time two places with the same name exist nearer Toulouse in the neighbourhood of Foix. Which of these two pairs do we have to choose? I do not think it is necessary to be too precise. All four places were situated in centres saturated with heresy. The Montgaillard south east of Carcassonne is situated in the Corbières, in the range of arid hills where the outlawed nobility put up their final resistance which terminated in the fall of the chateau of Queribus in 1255, that is to say eleven years after the surrender of Montségur.

Another very good reason for opting for the Montbrun and Montgaillard in the area east of Carcassonne is that Roger's friend, Mir de Camplong, lived in this area. Camplong is little more than fifty kilometres as the crow flies from Fanjeaux, the home of his friend Roger.

I have no conscious recollection of my part in the thirteenth century. At the same time the Corbières, the harsh, rocky hills which constitute the Eastern Pyrenees, affect me as no other countryside has ever done. The land seems living to me. I have similar though not so intense feelings about the undulating country which includes Montréal, Mazerolles and the other centres mentioned by Mrs. Smith. There are plenty of people writing books on reincarnation who would regard this as evidence but as I am approaching this thesis as an amateur historian I will content myself by calling it love of a particular kind of country combined with hindsight. But why did I suddenly feel mysteriously impelled by this kind of country in 1938 when I had always previously insisted on the high Alps and Alpine meadows?

The main argument in favour of Montbrun and Montgaillard being in the neighbourhood of Foix is that Mrs. Smith when she visited that area had a feeling of conscious familiarity with it. This fact is of predominating importance in view of the astonishing accuracy of her far memory as a whole. This applies also to Roger's appellation de Grisolles.[1] We have to accept it is probable that he had estates in the neighbourhood of Toulouse. Mrs.

[1] On October 3rd, 1969, Monsieur Duvernoy asked me whether I was certain that the fourth letter in this name was an S or an F. He said that in ancient manuscripts the two letters were difficult to distinguish from each other. This is an interesting point because in her first mention of this place in her letter of February 10th, 1966, Mrs. Smith said she did not know if she had written F or S. In Cassini's map, produced for military purposes for the King of France in the eighteenth century, a place described as Grefeilhe, now Aigrefeuille, and in the thirteenth century Grifoles, is to be found fifteen kilometres south-east of Toulouse. Monsieur Duvernoy pointed out that this does not affect the story because the whole area in the neighbourhood of Toulouse was saturated with Catharism.

Smith describes him as living in a house in that neighbourhood. It was also in that region that he first met Puerilia.

44

With regard to the period of our history, this is adequately established. The highlight of the story is, logically as well as historically, the massacre of the Inquisitors at Avignonet. After all, it was Pierre de Mazerolles' return from this which provided the substance for Mrs. Smith's principal recurrent nightmare. The massacre occurred in 1242. Roger was still free at this time and in his late fifties or early sixties. The deposition of Helis de Mazerolles and other sources made it quite clear that he and others of his generation, like Helis and Fabrissa, grew up in the last years of the twelfth and lived the greater part of their lives in the first half of the thirteenth century. Helis in her deposition refers to contacts with heretics as far back as 1195. She must have been young at this time.

It is unfortunate, but not surprising, that one does not know the exact date of Roger's death but to do so, after the lapse of seven centuries, would be to expect a little too much.

45

POEMS.

The immediately foregoing sections are the most important from the historical and psychological points of view. In them we have been able to test the validity of Mrs. Smith's experiences and to place them in their proper historical setting. The section to follow is fascinating in its own right but is of special interest to the student of literature. It is for this reason that the subject of poetry has been taken out of the main stream of the narrative and concentrated in one Section.

175

In one of his letters Professor Nelli asked if Mrs. Smith remembered any poetry from the thirteenth century. He pointed out that in those days people had, more than today, the capacity to remember what was recited or sung to them. I mentioned this request to Mrs. Smith. She replied in a letter dated March 29th, 1967, 'Yes, I have some poetry but only bits of what Roger used to say. I have written it in very bad modern French and in some cases it is in shorthand and in English. I didn't know much French at that time so I'm pretty certain that my translations are bad and inaccurate. At the moment my notes are in the loft covered by a pile of junk. When we get straightened out a bit I'll try to find the poetry.'

The poems arrived in two batches. Their provenance is interesting. After his death, a few were found, with her school reports, among a few special possessions her father kept in an old dispatch box. It seems extraordinary that her father, a non-commissioned soldier, should have kept so carefully poems in mediaeval French which from every rational point of view must have been Greek to him. Perhaps he, too, had far memory. He was very secretive about his recent French ancestry. Mrs. Smith only discovered after his death that she had French blood in her viens. It is very unfortunate that more poems were destroyed when his effects were disposed of.

Early in April 1967 I received a specimen of the poetry. Mrs. Smith commenced, 'Roger certainly believed in piling on the agony. This masterpiece has a second verse. I used to listen to it all starry eyed and I thought it was marvellous. That's what I call romance ! ! I've been laughing about it all the morning.

'The poem including the second verse is as under : —

> "Sous un castel qu'on appelle Mortier
> En point d'heure et au grand beau lever
> Les demoiselles y vont pour caracoler
> Si les escuyers y vont pour monter
> Si les chevaliers y vont pour regarder
> Vont y les dames pour leurs corps remuer

Ma belle Peirone s'y est fait mener
S'ils ont vetu un bliaut de cendal
Qui Grand Dieu entraine par les pres.
Je vous aime, vous n'aimez.

Si vienne Dieu les Maux sont remis
Florissent bois, les pres sont reverdis
Si vienne Paques les belles en Avril
Les douces nymphes rentraient a leur fil
Ma belle pucelle, acceptons la folie
Qui amour a, ne doit mettre en oublie
Souvent ill doit aller et venir
Je vous aime, vous m'aimez." '

Herewith my translation of the poem.

At the foot of the castle of Mortier
At dawn and sunset
The maidens go to wander up and down
And the squires to ride
And the Knights to watch
And the ladies go there to take the air
My lovely Peirone had someone to escort her
So they dressed in tunics of fine red silk
Those whom God leads through the pastures.
I love you, you love me.

May God come and our sins be forgiven
The woods are in blossom, the meadows are once more green
May Easter come, the beautiful ladies in April
The sweet nymphs returned to the flow of the river
My pretty maid, let us accept this madness
He who loves must not forget
It must come and go often
I love you, you love me.

Now what can we say of the origin of this poem? We can quite easily date it in time. In *French Lyrics*, selected and annotated by Professor George Saintsbury of Oxford and published in London in 1906, we find the following poem.[1] It is very similar to that remembered by Mrs. Smith. There are certain differences but the similarities are enough to classify it as belonging to the same period.

> Or vienent pasques les beles en avril
> Florissent bois, cil pre sont raverdi,
> Cez douces eves retraient a lor fil
> Cil oisel chantent au soir et au matin
> 'Qui amors a, nes doit metre en oubli
> Sovent i doit et aler et venir.'
> Ja s'entramoient Aigline et li quens Guis
> Guis aime Aigline, Aigline aime Guion.
>
> Souz un chastel q'en apele Biaucler
> En mout poi d'eure i ot granz bauz lever
> Ces demoiselles i vont por caroler,
> Cil escuier i vont por behorder,
> Cil chevalier i vont por esgander,
> Vont i cez dames por lor cors deporter
> La bele Aigline si est fete mener:
> Si ot vestu un bliant de cendel,
> Qui granz deus aures trainot par les prez
> Guis aime Aigline, Aigline aime Guion.

When was this poem written? Commenting on half a dozen lyrics, of which this is one, Saintsbury, a very great authority, says, 'The dates of these poems are not ascertainable exactly, but may be taken to be between 1150 and 1250. They are all anonymous except "L'Autrier en Mai", which is attributed to a certain Moniot d'Arras'.

This fits in exactly with Mrs. Smith's recollections. Roger's

---

[1] It is also to be found in Karl Bartsch's 'Alt Französische Romanzen und Pastourellen'.

life was lived in the first half of the thirteenth century. The poem could have been written in his day or just before it. Either way it fits in with Saintsbury's estimates.

There are certain differences to be noted in Mrs. Smith's and Saintsbury's versions. For a start the verses are in different order. Which is the correct version? For reasons which we will discover later it is difficult to speak of correct and incorrect versions of troubadour poems. All one can say is that Mrs. Smith's version is by far the most logical. Troubadour poems contain so often lines of religious import. The significance of the latter is often hidden. It is obvious in the poem under consideration. In the first verse of Mrs. Smith's version the characters concerned are mostly engaged in worldly occupations. The only line with any religious import is the ninth of the first verse. In the second verse the religious feeling is intensified. The last four lines could well have an esoteric meaning. This latter supposition is wild surmise. It is an undeniable feature of troubadour poetry that even what seems the most amorous has a hidden, religious meaning. One troubadour, referring to his own love poem, says 'Thou can'st go whither thou wilt. I have dressed thee so well that thou wilt be understood by those endowed with intelligence. Of others thou need'st not be concerned.'

To me the order of verses in Mrs. Smith's version makes more sense than that quoted by Professor Saintsbury.

Mrs. Smith recalls emphatically that the versions were sung in the order she has given.

Perhaps the most crucial difference between the poems is that Mrs. Smith's contains a line not present in Saintsbury's version. This is the opening line of her second verse. '*Si vienne Dieu les maux sont remis*', meaning '*May God come and our sins be forgiven.*' Why is this absent in Saintsbury's version and present in Mrs. Smith's? This is a complete and exciting mystery. We know that this poem was written between 1150 and 1250. Did it come, after all, before the version heard by Mrs. Smith? Did Roger have a feeling of guilt about her? Did he add the first line or was it just another expression of his deep, religious

179

feeling? We cannot know but this added line poses a fascinating problem.

The next significant difference is that no men's names are mentioned in Mrs. Smith's poem. We only hear of Peirone.[2] In Saintsbury's version the names of both lovers are mentioned. The name also of the castle is different. This is easy enough to follow. Troubadours adapted their poems to suit their audiences. No doubt there was an Aigiline and a Guis in those who listened to the troubadour responsible for the Saintsbury version. No doubt the entertainment took place in a castle called Biaucler.

There are also inevitably differences of spelling in the two versions. In the Middle Ages writers were more free with alternative methods of spelling. It is interesting that in the Saintsbury rendering *eves* is substituted for *nymphs*. I suspect that the reference to *nymphs* or *eves* going back to their *fil* is of religious significance. Certainly *fil* is to be read as course of a river and has nothing to do with spinning. It must also be accepted that *eve*, like *aigue*, conveys in old French the flow of water.

We have said that very often there is a hidden religious meaning in troubadour poems. In the poem we have discussed we have eight lines in which people are at their ease and behaving frivolously. Why the sudden reference in the ninth line to those whom God leads through the pastures? Is the red silken tunic referred to in the previous line the symbolisation of a garment of spiritual significance? Because of these factors, and considering that Mrs. Smith's second verse has such an unmistakably religious opening, is the phrase 'I love you, you love me' which comes at the end of each verse, necessarily to be accepted as a mere statement of human love?

Why was Mrs. Smith able to produce these poems? At thirteen she was very emphatically not taught mediaeval French with phrases in the Langue d'Oc[3] in her local grammar school. One cannot fall back on general explanations like inspiration. At a

[2] Feminine version of Peire, Pierre (Peter).
[3] See later.

pinch a girl of this age could be inspired to write poetry in a foreign language though hardly of this quality. It is quite impossible, however, to regard her as having a specific inspiration to write in the Langue d'Oc and in mediaeval French. Her knowledge of the latter is even now negligible. In the letter accompanying the poem already quoted she asked 'What, for instance, is an escuyer?' This is the old spelling of ecuyer which means squire i.e. to a knight. It requires no knowledge of mediaeval French to know that in many modern French words the S has been dropped, for example, that *estait* has become *etait*. She even expressed surprise that she had written *vous* as *vos*. You do not have to know much French, let alone the mediaeval variety, to know that this was the former usage.

On April 27th she wrote deploring the fact that she learnt French before recording her experiences. Referring specifically to the poetry she said, 'I'm sure I mucked the poetry about by writing it in modern French. I don't know any old French at all but it would have been far more interesting had I written some.' Clearly she did not realise even at this late date that mediaeval French and Langue d'Oc had found its way into her poems. She wrote, 'Some of the French is so peculiar and I can't make much sense of it.'

This poem and the others must have come to her by a mixture of clair-audience and far memory. In July 1969 I wrote her a letter about the absence of punctuation in her poems. On July 29th, 1969, she wrote back replying to my question and also enlightening me as to the mode of transmission of the poems. 'As far as punctuation goes, I'm afraid I can be of very little help for I haven't the slightest notion whether I wrote the poems without punctuation because that's how they came over, or because I felt there was no need, or indeed if I left it out from sheer laziness or ignorance. It was all so long ago and honestly I can't remember. The only sure thing about the whole subject is that
a) I wrote them with great ease.
b) I had never studied old French at the time they were written and at that period of my life I could scarcely write modern

French. I was never taught the former and have *never* studied it in later years either.'

It should be made clear that at the time of writing Mrs. Smith has no accurate recollection of the poems she took down as a girl. She handed over to me what was left of the original script. She certainly cannot be said to be obsessed by this aspect of her experience. When she saw the Saintsbury version of her poem, 'Sous un Castel' she described it in a letter of August 14th 1969 as 'vaguely familiar' and added, 'I haven't a copy of the one I wrote so I'm not really in a position to compare it.' This is analogous to those mediums who do not know the content of the messages they have transmitted.

She set little store by the poetry and it was only interesting to her because it was sung by Roger. This year, in re-reading it and other mediaeval lyrics of the same period, she is prepared to admit that it has charm.

The second poem, like all those to follow, is also on the theme of love.

POEM 2.

Si Beles ieuz, vairs et plaisons,
Plein de tres desbonaire ris
Me font amer si loyaument
Qui merveille est que je sois vif
Son corps vaut bien un paradis
Que veoir la pourrait souvent
Mais je vos dis veraiement
Que trop en suis arriere mis
Si m'en dement.'

Herewith my translation.

Such lovely eyes, changing and seductive
So rich in ceaseless laughter
Arouse in me a love so constant
That I marvel that I still live

To those who see her often
Her body is indeed a paradise
But I tell you truly
I am so abandoned
That my mind sickens

This little poem has a sharp and concise beauty which it is impossible to convey in English. Anyone with any knowledge of French will see that, while I maintain that I have extracted correctly the essence of the poem, I have not given a strictly literal translation of it. Neither have I done so in the case of the other poems. I have regarded these as being sufficiently beautiful to impose on me the duty of rendering them as felicitously as possible in English, within the limits imposed by my modest powers.

The next poem is Mrs. Smith's favourite. It is small, beautiful and jewelled. One cannot convey its polished effect in translation. In sending it to me she said, 'I can't make much sense of this but it is possibly the most interesting of all the bits and pieces we have. Strange that the only ones I write in old French were in my father's possession. I'll never know why he kept them. It was in a very messy state when I found it—covered with a lot of scribbling and drawings in green pencil. I was interested to see I spelt Roger "Rogier". I haven't done so elsewhere.'

POEM 3.

Je vos ameroie Rogier
Et vos mi donroie
Senture ferree d'argent
Jhesus ke ferai?
Je voi bien tuit perdu ai

Dieus con si ait biauz bois
Li rosignors i chante
La mavis la callandre
Li orious tuit li oisel ki sont

Ou bois sor la violete
Ki tant ait doucete
Et jone pucelete
Suis si pris
Tuit fis la foliete
La soie merci.
Reposon nous.

Herewith the translation of poem 3. In this poem I give alternative versions for the second half of the second verse. My reasons for so doing will be given immediately after each translation.

I shall love you Roger
And you will give me
A silver-studded girdle
Jesus, what shall I do?
Truly I see all I had is lost

God how beautiful the woods are
Here the nightingales sing
The redwings, the larks
The orioles and all the choir of birds
In the trees above the violets
Which have such sweetness
And the young maidens
So close to me
Play like children
Lost in their hearts' content
Let us rest.

There is no doubt about it that this poem is difficult to translate. It is like hacking a diamond out of coal. In translating this, and the other poems, there are certain points we must bear in mind. Firstly, in mediaeval French and the Langue d'Oc, the meaning of some words and phrases is a matter of conjecture,
184

even to the specialists. Secondly, one has to struggle with the extremely condensed form of troubadour poems. They had to be written within the limits of certain conventions. The poet had to pack his meaning, often esoteric in nature, into a small, pre-fabricated structure. Thirdly, it must be remembered that to some extent Mrs. Smith's recording of these poems is phonetic. She is taking them down by ear. For her the nightingales 'chante'. They do not 'chantent' because the ending 'ent' is not pronounced in French.

In my first version of the second verse I am translating the phrase *Tuit fis la foliete*, regarding *foliete* as the operative word, to convey that everybody is fooling about. But equally one can say that the previous line *'Suis si pris'* means I am taken, that is to say, possessed in love. Now *foliete* is also the Provencal word for foliage, in which case *'La soie merci'* is an expression of thankfulness for the cover afforded by the trees. It is clear from the first verse that she and Roger have been making love. It is not likely that there would have been other maidens in the vicinity. The love-making habits of thirteenth century Languedoc were more refined than those of modern Britain. I therefore submit the following as an alternative translation for the second verse.

> God how beautiful the woods are
> Here the nightingales sing
> The redwing, the larks
> The orioles and all the choir of birds
> In the trees above the violets
> Which have such sweetness
> I, in the gentleness of maidenhood
> Am thus possessed
> All is shadow under the leaves
> Let us be thankful and rest.

At this stage we have an exciting discovery. Knowing that I was writing a section on these poems, Mrs. Smith searched in her local library to see if she could discover any of the six pieces she had taken down, rather as a spiritualist medium might operate, a quarter of a century earlier. She succeeded in unearthing Abbott's *Early Mediaeval French Lyrics* but missed one tiny passage of great interest. It comes in the fourth verse of poem 50 in the collection. This poem is classified as a *pastourelle* of Picard origin. The passage runs : —

> *Je vos ameroie*
> *belle, et si vos donroie*
> *Senture ferre d'argent.*

This is the sole likeness to Mrs. Smith's poem in this *pastourelle* of five verses each of eight lines. The difference is that the Roger of Mrs. Smith's poem is not mentioned. One finds instead in the refrain in each verse the name Robeson translated as Robin. Once again we may draw the conclusion that the name was inserted to suit the audience which may have included someone of the name of Robeson. Alternatively a person of that name may have been well-known to the people present.

But why, as in Mrs. Smith's poem, the repetition of

> *si vos donroie*
> *senture ferre d'argent.*

The silver studded girdle could well be something of esoteric significance. In the thirteenth century it was widely held that Cathar Parfaits wore a mysterious girdle next to their skin but it is probable that this was only a Catholic superstition.

This poem, almost in its entirety, was discovered for me by a French friend in Paul Meyer's *Recueil d'Anciens Textes*, and handed to me on October 7th, 1969. The poem is by Raimbaut de Vacqueiras. This troubadour is mentioned at least six times in Professor Nelli's classic, *L'Erotique des Troubadours*. The period coincides perfectly, 1155-1205. Roger with his troubadour interests and background, must have been familiar with his poetry.

As so often occurs in troubadour poetry one finds an alternative version of the second verse of the poem as quoted by Meyer. This verse ends:—

> Ki tant est sadete
> la pucelete
> Suis si pris
> Dous ami
> Reposon nous.

Sadate, meaning pleasant, delightful, etc, is used instead of doucete as in Mrs. Smith's version. There is no adjective with pucelete (maiden) and, 'Tuit fis la foliete', is missed out. The poem is, however, beyond any doubt essentially the same as Mrs. Smith's favourite.

Mademoiselle Lamé, who found this poem for me in Meyer's collection, points out that, 'Suis si pris', can be translated, 'I am near', as well as, 'I am taken'.

The fourth poem Mrs. Smith regards with affection and disdain. Roger used to sing it but she does not think he wrote it, 'because it was sung in many places by different people'. She dismisses it as a thirteenth-century pop song. She sent it to me under this title. She wrote of it, 'Mediaeval pop songs weren't any better than the ones we have today'. I do not agree with her, though I do not care for this poem as much as for the others.

POEM 4.

> Amie, mon envie
> Est gente, bellette,
> Jeunette, gentillette
> Pour si doux plaisir.
> Votre bouchette
> Vermeillette,
> Riante et amoureuse
> M'en donne desir
> Votre manierette

> *Doucette,*
> *Simple, plaisante, joliette,*
> *M'en donne desir.*

My translation is as follows:

> *My love, sweet goal of my desire*
> *You are gentle, beautiful*
> *Young and kind*
> *For such deep joy*
> *Your little mouth like a rose*
> *Laughing and loving*
> *Awakens my desire*
> *Your tender eyes*
> *Simple, charming and appealing*
> *Awaken my desire.*

The number of diminutives ending in *ette* in this poem are characteristic of troubadour poetry. They are also typical of early French mediaeval verse, though in the latter such forms tend to occur somewhat later than the period of which we are writing. This is easy to understand since troubadour poetry was a pioneer development as far as European civilisation was concerned. Nevertheless they do occur in French mediaeval verse as early as the first half of the thirteenth century. A poem by Colin Muset, who lived in the east of France in the first half of the thirteenth century, illustrates clearly this passion for diminutives and for ending consecutive lines with them.

Muset's poem is as follows:

> *Sospris sui d'une amorette.*
> *D'une jone pucelette*
> *bel est et blonde et blanchette*
> *Plus que n'est une erminette*
> *Sa la color vermeillette*
> *Ensi com une rosette.*

In a letter of July 22nd, 1969, Mrs. Smith reveals her constant scrupulousness and capacity for self-criticism. She is also always allowing for explanations other than far memory to account for what was revealed to her. Her letter says, 'It's clear that most of the poems are the same type as Roger's—love and religion being the main themes. The pop song, for instance—any one of those following sound awfully like it.' She then quotes Muset's poem and two others. These similarities are all the more evidence of the truth of her experiences. They are convincing evidence to prove that the songs sung by Roger were genuine troubadour poetry of the thirteenth century.

There is, however, still better to come. In Saintsbury's French Lyrics we find a poem of Jehannot de Lescurel entitled Love's Reasons and containing phrases almost identical with those in Mrs. Smith's pop song. Compare de Lescurel's

> 'Car vo bouchette
> Vermeillette
> Rians et amoureusette
> Fait que, sans partir.' with Mrs. Smith's
> 'Votre bouchette
> Vermeillette,
> Riante et amoureuse
> M'en donne desire.'

In another verse of de Lescurel's the comparison is closer still

> 'Vo manierette
> Joliette,
> Simple, plaisans, faitissette
> M'en donne desir.'

Compare this with Mrs. Smith's

> 'Votre manierette,
> Doucette,
> Simple, plaisante, joliette
> M'en donne desir.'

Commenting on de Lescurel, Professor Saintsbury says, 'The date and personality of Jehannot de Lescurel are quite unknown, but the former must have been about the first half of the fourteenth century. His poems have great sweetness and melody. The second (i.e. *Love's Reasons* from which I have quoted) displays a lavishness in diminutives which continued to be a characteristic of French poetry until the occultation of the Pléiade).'

The first half of the fourteenth century is too late for Roger but Saintsbury's estimation is only approximate but this does not affect the issue. Once again we have the phenomenon of one author borrowing from another and the transposition of what seems almost to be set forms from one poem to another. Amendments and readaptations of the same poems went on for at least a century. Mrs. Smith, in her letter of July 29th 1969, quoted Abbott as saying, 'There were many versifiers who for profit or reputation wrote at second hand. This is a malady not confined to troubadours.'

What Roger sang could well have been an earlier edition of de Lescurel's poem. We must always remember that the poetry of the troubadours of the Languedoc and Provence preceded that of poets elsewhere in France. At any rate we have once again an example of the troubadour addiction to diminutives.

The fifth specimen is a charming love poem. Of its nine lines, eight end in *er*. The use of such set forms is typical of troubadour poetry.

> *Amie, la nuit je me mais rêvasser*
> *En dormant vous crus embrasser*
> *Et quand je le fais au reveil*
> *Nul rien ne m'y put aider*
> *Lors me reprends a vous souhaiter.*
>
> *Belle douce amie, ne vous sais louanger*
> *Mais de fin de coeur je vous aime et sans tricher*
> *Quand vous plaira, si me pourrez baiser*
> *Entre vos bras me vouloir aller coucher.*

The translation is as follows:

> My love, I know that in the night in dreams
> I felt in sleep my arms about you
> And then, awakening, I again enfold you
> With the return of my longing
> Nothing calms my pain
> Sweet and gentle lady, to praise you is beyond me.
> But from the depth of my heart I love you sincerely
> When it moves you to kiss me
> I will wish again to sleep in your arms.

In the translations I have inserted here and there a less than minimal punctuation for the sake of clarity. As presented to me by Mrs. Smith punctuation was almost non-existent. I have also, on one or two occasions, changed the order of the lines, because, in so doing, the poems read better in English.

The sixth poem is worthy of special attention. Parts of it are superb. It is longer than the others, less of this world and its religious content is clear and obvious. It poses achingly the conflict between the flesh and the spirit in the heart of a lover of priestly vocation. This poem is of more personal interest to us because Mrs. Smith is especially concerned with it because it contains a place name. Once she had decided to tell her story she was always preoccupied with where she had lived and with the verification of names of places and of individuals.

This poem contains the lines

> 'Bon Grand Dieu par égard pour vos
> Quitte Terride on est celle qui j'aime si.'

In these lines the poet is deploring the fact that he has to leave Terride. Mrs. Smith wrote me on April 25th, 1967, to say that she felt that at one time she was living somewhere south of Foix, near Montbrun. This was in the area of the Montgaillard (not the place in the Eastern Pyrenees) where she had a definite feeling of recall when she visited it. She felt that she left this place to go and live elsewhere with Roger. She wondered where

191

she went on this occasion and thought this place might be Terride 'if', as she continued in her letter, 'such a place exists but I can't see it on the map. It would be marvellous if I could discover a place Terride near Fanjeaux but I haven't such hope'.

Shortly afterwards I had another letter from her. She was disappointed that her enquiries in France had produced no news of Terride. She had found out that there must have been an estate of Terride 700 years ago because there was at that time an Arnaud, Vicomté de Terride et de Gimoes. He took the surname of Verdun, which is very near Grisolles. Mrs. Smith need not have been disappointed. She was later proved to be right. I learnt early in 1968 from Monsieur Duvernoy that Terride was actually in the Mirepoix estate. The word Terride seems to have been used early in history in the thirteenth century or even before. Don Vaissette's *L'Histoire de Languedoc* mentions a chateau of that name. Terride was also used later in history after the Albigensian crusades, when the estates of the Cathar lords of Mirepoix had passed into the hands of the usurping de Levis family.

Mrs. Smith said it would be marvellous but more than she hoped if she could find a place Terride near Fanjeaux. The distance as the crow flies between Terride-Mirepoix and Fanjeaux is about seventeen kilometres. In Adelin Moulis' book *L'Ariege et ses Chateaux Feodaux*, chapter VIII, entitled 'Canton de Mirepoix', the sub-title is 'Mirepoix or Terride'. Opposite page 98 of the same work there is a photograph with the title 'Mirepoix: remains of the chapel of the chateau of Terride.'

POEM 6

Douce amie, j'ai au coeur grande douleur
Quand il convient enfin de vos partir
Chez qui j'ai trouvé tant de grâce, tant de douceur
Joie et confort, tout à mon plaisir
Mais la fortune a fait par sa puissance
Changer ma joie en tristesse et en pénitence
Que souffrirai pour vos mainte nuit et maint jour

Ainsi je dois servir mon Créateur
Mais je n'ai pas en moi tant d'abstinence
Cent fois la nuit je me rappelle vostre semblance
Tant je me plais à vostre corps tenir
Quand me l'aurai pas je mourrai de désir
Bon grand Dieu par égard pour vos
Quitte Terride où est celle que j'aime si
Vos nous accordez en ciel joie à toujours
M'amie et moi par la vostre merci
Et lui accordez de moi amour puissance
Pour qu'elle ne m'oublit pas durant ma longue absence
Car je l'aime plus que rien qui soit au monde
J'en ai de la peine tel que le coeur m'en fond
Belle Peirone, pour tout Dieu vos commande
Je ne puis plus avec vos demeurer
Je dois pour l'amour de Dieu aller
Pour sauver les âmes je vais en bonne entente
Mais sachez bien, amie belle et gente
Que tout comme fleur nâit de l'ente
Nâit le grand désir de vos qui me tourmente
Quand s'en revient douce amie, je puis jurer
Que c'est pour vos garder et honorer.

Herewith the translation of Poem 6.
Sweet lady, my heart has a deep pain
In this hour of farewell
To one in whom I found such grace and sweetness
Such joy and comfort to the limits of my longing
But the malice of fortune
Has changed my joy into sadness and penitence
So for you I shall suffer many nights and days
For thus I must serve my Creator
But I had not within me such denial of myself
And with the night I summon endlessly your image
I so delight in your body's embrace
That in its absence I will die of longing

Almighty God, it is for You
I leave Terride and she whom I adore
May you grant unending joy in heaven
By your grace to my lady and me
So that she forget me not in my long absence
For I love her more than all things on earth
I suffer such pain that my heart breaks
Beautiful Peirone, though God is your guide
I can no more stay with you
For the love of God I must away
To save the souls of others, I go in peace
But know, beautiful and gentle lady
That as a flower is born of its bud
So rises the yearning for you which torments me
When I return, sweet friend, I swear
It is to keep you always and to offer you reverence.

This poem appears to me the most impressive of all. It may lack the lyrical quality of *Amie, la nuit je me sais revasser* but as an expression of a man's struggle with himself it is convincing as well as beautiful. If it seems that some of the sentiments expressed are trite—and they do not seem so to me—one should reflect that such poetry was produced in the thirteenth century. Where else in Europe at this time was such poetry being produced? In other European civilisations the verse at this period, in comparison with troubadour poetry, resembles the first lumbering steps of a cart horse pitted against the supple but disciplined movements of a thoroughbred.

In one of her letters, Mrs. Smith made the following comments on this poem. 'It's a bit on the religious side—about saving souls and leaving me because of his duty to his Creator ! ! He called me Puerilia but Peirone is mentioned several times in the songs or poems or whatever one might call them.'

Peirone was among the common female names in thirteenth-century Languedoc. Guiraud refers to a Parfaite called Peirona (or Peirone) de la Mote. There is also a reference elsewhere to a woman called Peirone and her daughter, both of whom suffered at the hands of the Inquisition.

The proliferation of diminutives, the common endings, mostly *er*, to most of the lines, the general form of the poems and the discovery that fragments of them are repeated in early French lyrics from other sources, establishes these poems as troubadour products of the thirteenth century. We have also further evidence as to their origin.

The use of *ki* for the modern French *qui* and *ke* for *que* help us to place the poems in the twelfth and thirteenth centuries. *Ki* and *ke* occur in the version of the *Chanson de Rolande*, described as Manuscript Digby 23 in the Bodleian Library at Oxford. This manuscript was written in the twelfth century. Its language is described by its editor, F. Whitehead, as western French of the early twelfth century. Certainly the date of our story is later but there is no need to assume that usages such as *ki* and *ke* lasted no more than a century. Also we should remember that Roger was singing songs not necessarily of his own day.

In Mrs. Smith's poems Jesus and Roger are spelt *Jhesus* and *Rogier*. These are Langue d'Oc forms of spelling but could also be old French. In the poems there are other nouns with archaic spellings. *Rosignor*, meaning nightingale, modern French rosignol, is a variation of the old Provencal standard form *rosinhol* but alternative forms ending in *or* are also possible in old Catalan and French. Similarly *tuit* is a Provencal variation of *tots* i.e. *tous*, meaning all, but also occurs in old French.

In Mrs. Smith's poems, where there is an archaic form which can be considered either Langue d'Oc or old French, we must opt for the former. This is because, quite apart from these poems, in her schoolgirl notes Mrs. Smith wrote *meire* for mere (mother) and in her first reference to Pierre de Mazerolles his Christian name is spelt *Peire*. In *Meire* and *Peire* she is clearly using her native tongue. It is therefore reasonable to assume that the archaic usages in her poems are Langue d'Oc rather than old French. It was not for nothing that I was directed at the beginning of this story to Mr. H's house where I first met the Tibetan

Lama and where I rang a bell in my memory by picking up a copy of Fernard Niel's *Albigeois et Cathares*. Why should Mr. H., of all things a physics master at a public school, have taught himself Provencal years previously?

One of the most striking relics of the Langue d'Oc in Mrs. Smith's poems is the word *foliete*, meaning foliage in English. The word in Provencal is *folhet*. In French it would be *verdure*. The word *caracoler* which occurs in *Sous un castle qu'on appele Mortier* is also interesting. This means to stroll about and is Catalan in origin. As such it would be in use in the Languedoc in the early Middle Ages.

It cannot be doubted that these are troubadour poems from the thirteenth century. We know that Fabrissa de Mazerolles, Blanche de Laurac and others were well-known protectors of Cathars. It is accepted that the great houses noted for their sympathy to Catharism were essentially those which were also hospitable to troubadours. It is beyond the scope of this book to discuss to what degree Catharism and the philosophy embodied in many of the troubadour poems were related to each other, but that such a connection existed cannot be doubted.

In this story we have no need to labour the question of the affinities between troubadour poetry and Cathar doctrine and philosophy. We know already that Guillaume de Durfort, the ruins of whose castle my wife and I stumbled on, as it were by accident, was both a practising Cathar and a troubadour poet. It is usually said that probably four or five of the famous troubadours were Cathars but the exacting judgement of Professor Nelli only allows this double qualification to be truly established in the single case of Guillaume of Durfort. This man was Roger's grandfather. Of all the families in the Languedoc, Roger's was, more than any other, so endowed as to offer him a golden opportunity to express both his poetical interests and his Catharism.

It is almost certain that the poems transmitted through Mrs. Smith were popular tunes of their day. (I have a feeling that *Douce Amie* does not come into this category and that its origin is different but in saying this I am relying on intuition rather than concrete evidence.) Mrs. Smith holds this opinion. On August 3rd, 1969, she writes, 'Were Roger's poems/songs popular ballads of the day? The fact that names and places are different is quite unimportant.' (She is referring to differences observed in the poems collected by Abbott and Saintsbury.) 'People could quite easily have changed these things to suit themselves. That would explain too why in many poems the same line occurs. After all, one finds this in popular ballads of today—I mean "the moon is blue and I am too" sort of thing. If I hear a sentimental ballad I frequently find no difficulty at all in singing some of the lines or humming the melody without having previously heard the song. This isn't because I am very clever, but solely because the tunes are often very similar to other songs I've already heard, and the words form a set pattern and are fairly obvious.' Anybody familiar with troubadour poems of the twelfth and thirteenth centuries will know what she means by set patterns.

The above paragraph contains Mrs. Smith's opinions. What is more important to us are her memories. So far as the authorship of any poetry is concerned, she is certain that she never saw Roger in the act of writing. She has other facts to impart of even greater interest. In a letter dated August 3rd, 1969, she writes, 'The years have dulled my memory and I can't now recall any of the tunes. Years ago I sometimes found myself humming "Roger's tunes" and if other people were around the effect was always the same—a request to sing something with more rhythm and tune to it!!! I say without vanity that I sang well as a girl,[4] so it's a pretty safe bet that I was reproducing those tunes exactly as I remembered them and yet those songs came over as miserable dirges. I wonder why. One would think the troubadours would have produced tunes easily recalled, easy to sing, easy to dance to. I wonder if the words were more important than the melody.'

My second daughter, a teacher of music by profession, tells

[4] She used to sing in public.

me that such troubadour music as she has heard is, by our standards, melancholy and monotonous. I feel that Mrs. Smith is right as usual. Certainly what she says about the words being more important than the melody cannot be gainsaid. This is inevitably so, seeing that so many troubadour poems were of the nature of riddles and designed to have a hidden meaning.

I wish it were possible to be more precise as to the authorship of all these poems. They may in part have been the work of poets contemporary with Roger. And of course we must not leave Roger's grandfather, Guillaume de Durfort, out of the reckoning. It is not reasonable on the evidence to hazard even a guess but he may well be a likely candidate for the honour.

To reflect on the authorship of these poems is absorbing but it is more fascinating to recall how they were transmitted. *Si beles ieuz* is written on the back of a report made on Mrs. Smith's work by her history teacher. Did the latter realise that Mrs. Smith was busy on another history? *Je vos ameroie Rogier* decorates the reverse side of a printed document headed, 'English —Progress Test No. 12.' This instructive missive requests the pupil to refer to the works in which the following characters occur and to state the author's name in each case. The characters are Mr. Pesksniff, Lady Psyche, Macduff, Prospero, Touchstone, Laertes and Amyas Leigh. Not very advanced stuff, but suitable for a girl in her early teens. I wonder what the authorities would have thought had they discovered Mrs. Smith at her other occupation.

BIBLIOGRAPHY

This bibliography is by no means complete. The works mentioned are also of uneven quality. The better contemporary authorities are more to be relied on than the works of their eminent precursors. For instance, while Guiraud's History of the Inquisition in the Middle Ages is deservedly regarded as a work of reference, it contains, as noted by Duvernoy, numerous errors of fact. Its faults in interpretation, due to the author's non-intuitive approach to Catharism, are clearly evident.

Among the mass of contemporary literature on Catharism the names of Nelli, Duvernoy and Roché are pre-eminent. Nelli is probably the greatest living exponent of the metaphysics of Catharism as well as being a renowned authority on Troubadour poetry. Roché is more concerned with the transcendental aspects of Catharism and its affiliations with the philosophy of Manichæism and of the Early Christian Gnostic fathers such as Origen. He is also the moving spirit behind the invaluable quarterly *Cahiers d'Etudes Cathares*. Duvernoy is outstandingly the most reliable authority on the basic history of Catharism and his methodical dissection of original documents has added greatly to our knowledge. Works by these three gentlemen are included in the bibliography and are to be recommended above all others.

Of earlier writers, as well as Guiraud one can recommend Lea's *History of the Inquisition in the Middle Ages*, and C. Schmidt's *Histoire et Doctrine de la Secte des Cathares ou Albigeois*.

There is no reasonably full and informative history of Catharism known to me in English. There are books on Dualism in general and Manichæism in particular but none especially devoted to the Cathars. The latter are, however, treated accur-

199

ately and intuitively in *The Holy Heretics* by Edmond Holmes, a clear-headed and elegant writer with good insight into the subject matter of his study, but unfortunately little known.

The reader is advised to approach with caution contemporary works of fiction with Catharism as their theme. Some of these are built on gross and often perverse misconceptions of the philosophy and aims of the Cathars. Zöe Oldenbourg's popular works are excellent.

ABBOTT, CLAUDE. *Early Mediaeval French Lyrics.* Kegan Paul, London, 1906.

ALLIX, PETER. *Remarks upon the Ecclesiastical History of the Ancient Churches of the Albigenses.* London, 1692 (later edition, Oxford, Clarendon Press, 1821).

ANON. *Chanson de la Croisade Albigeoise.* (See Guillaume de Tudele.)

Chanson de Rolande. Manuscript 23 Digby, Bodleian Library, Oxford.

BAYLEY, HAROLD. *The Lost Language of Symbolism.* Williams and Norgate, London, 1951.

A New Light on the Renaissance. Dent, London, 1900.

BARTSCH, KARL. *Alt Französische Romanzen und Pastourellen.*

BEC, PIERRE. *La Langue Occitane.* (In the series Que sais-je?)

BECK, JEAN. *Transcription of Des Chansons du Chansonniers Cangé.* Manuscript Francais No. 846 Bibliothèque Nationale de Paris.

BELL, VICARS. *Little Gaddesden.* Faber and Faber, London, 1949.

BELPERRON, PIERRE. *La Croisade Contre les Albigeois et l'Union de Languedoc a la France 1209-1249.*

BERGIN, *see* HILL and BERGIN.

BURKITT, F. C. *The Religion of the Manichees.*

CAHIERS DE FANJEAUX. *No. 3 Cathares en Languedoc.* Privat, Toulouse, 1968.

CAMPROUX, CHARLES. *Le Joy D'Amor des Troubadours.* Causse & Castelnau, Montpellier, 1965.

CLOSS, HANNAH. *The Albigensian Trilogy—High are the Moun-*

tains: Deep are the Valleys: The Silent Tarn. Vanguard Press, New York, 1962-63.

DANDO, MARCEL. *Les Origines du Catharisme*. Les Editions du Pavillon. Paris, 1967.

DE PUYLAURENS, GUILLAUME. *Chronique sur la Guerre des Albigeois*.

DE ROUGEMONT, DENIS. *L'Amour et L'Occident*. Union Generale d'Editions. Paris, 1963.

DE SÈDE, GÉRARD. *Le Trésor Cathare*. Juillard, Paris, 1966.

[1] DE TUDELE, GUILLAUME. Chanson de la Croisade Albigeoise, Martin-Chabot, 1931-1954.

DE VAULX-CERNAY, PIERRE. Histoire de l'Heresie des Albigeois.

DURBAN, PIERRE. *Actualité du Catharisme*. Cercle d'Etudes et Recherches de Psychologue Analytique, 1968.

DUVERNOY, JEAN. *Albigeisme ou Catharisme*. Cahiers du Sud, Nos. 387-388, 1966.

Les Albigeois dans la Vie Sociale et Economique de leurs temps. Bertrand Marty. Cahiers d'Etudes Cathares. Aut. 1968.

L'Exégèse Cathare de Jean. 3-4. Cahiers d'Etudes Cathares, Hiver, 1968-69.

Guilhabert de Castres. Cahiers d'Etudes Cathares, Été, 1967.

Inquisition à Pamiers. Privat, Toulouse, 1966.

La Liturgie et l'Eglise Cathares. Cahiers d'Etudes Cathares. Printemps, 1967.

Le Registre d'Inquisition de Jacques Fournier. Privat, Toulouse, 1968.

EPTON, NINA. *The Valley of the Pyrene*.

FORNAIRON, ERNEST. *Le Mystère Cathare*. Flammarion, Paris, 1964.

GENRICH, F. *Rondeaux, Virelais und Balladen*. Dresden, 1921.

GIROU, JEAN. *Carcassonne*. Arthaud, Grenoble, 1930.

GOUGAUD, HENRI. *Poèmes Politiques des Troubadours*. Bélibaste, Paris, 1969.

GRISART, M. *Le Catharisme dans le nord de la France*.

---

[1] Guillaume de Tudele wrote only part of Chanson de la Croisade. The latter portion was written by a more gifted anonymous author.

GUIRAUD, JEAN. *Cartulaire de Notre Dame de Prouille.*
Histoire de l'Inquisition au Moyen Age.

HANNEDOUCHE, S. *Le Roman Spirituel de Balaam et Josaphat.* Cahiers d'Etudes Cathares, Winter, 1967, Spring, 1968.

HILL and BERGIN. *Anthology of the Provencal Troubadours.* Yale University, 1941.

HOLMES, EDMOND. *The Holy Heretics.* Watts, London, 1948.

INGE, DEAN. *Mysticism.*

KEMP, P. *Healing Ritual.* Faber, 1935.

LEA, H. C. *History of the Inquisition in the Middle Ages.* (French translation. Reinach, Paris, 1900-1902.)

LEQUENNE, F. *Le Drame Cathare.* Paris, 1954.

LUCHAIRE, ACHILLE. *La Croisade des Albigeois.* Paris, 1905.

MADAULE, JACQUES. *Le Drame Albigeois et le destin Francais.*

MAGRE, MAURICE. *Magiciens et Illuminés.*

MARTIN. *Histoire de France.*

MEYER, PAUL. *Recuil d'Anciens Textes.*

MICHEL, AIMÉ. *La France Secrète.* La France qui dit non. Editions Planète, 1968.

MICHELET. *History of France.*

MILLET, GABRIEL. *La Religion Orthodoxe et les Heresies chez les Yougoslaves.* (Revue de l'Histoire des Religions.)

MOLINIER, CHARLES. *Coutume Religieuse des Derniers Sectaires Albigeois.* Bordeaux, 1881.
L'Inquisition dans le Midi de la France.

MONTGAILLARD, DESAZARS DE. *Histoire Authentique des Inquisiteurs tués à Avignonet en 1242.* Toulouse, 1869.

MOULIS, ADELIN. *L'Ariège et ses Chateaux Feodaux.* Edition de l'Auteur, 1968.
Montségur et le drame Cathare. Edition de l'auteur, 1968.

NATAF, ANDRÉ. *Le Miracle Cathare.* Robert Laffont, Paris, 1968.

NELLI, RENÉ. *Le Catharisme vu à travers les Tròubadours.* Cahiers de Fanjeaux, Privat, 1968.
Écritures Cathares. Editions Planète, Paris, 1968.
L'Érotique des Troubadours. Privat, Toulouse, 1903.
Itinéraire de la France Cathare. Editions Planète, 1968.

Le Musée du Catharisme. Privat, Toulouse, 1966.

La Nature Maligne dans le Dualisme Cathare du XIIIme siècle de l'Inégalité des Deux Principes. Editions de la Revue Folklore, 1969.

Le Phénomène Cathare. Privat. Toulouse, 1964.

Reflexions sur le Dualisme Cathare. Cahiers du Sud, Nos. 387, 388.

Le Rituel Cathare.

La Vie Quotidienne des Cathares. Hachette, Paris, 1969.

NIEL, FERNAND. *Albigeois et Cathares.* Presses Univ. de France, 1955.

La Dernière Nuit de Montségur. Cahiers du Sud, Nos. 387, 388.

Montsègur. Le Site, Son Histoire. Imprimerie Allier, Grenoble, 1962.

OBOLENSKY, D. *The Bogomils.* Cambridge, 1948.

OLDENBOURG, ZOË. *Le Bûcher de Montségur.* Gallimard, 1959.

PALAIS, SIMONE COINCY-SAINT. *Donjons et Castels au Pays des Cathares.*

PEIRE-CHABERT. *Actualité du Catharisme.* Editions Crux de Lux, Toulouse, 1961.

PELHISSON, GUILLAUME. *Chronique de Archives Romanes.* Traduite et commentée par Jean Duvernoy. Ousset, Toulouse, 1958.

PERRIN, JEAN-PAUL. *Histoire des Chrestiens Albigeois.* Genève, 1618.

PEYRAT, NAPOLEON. *Histoire Generale des Albigeois.* Paris, 1880.

RAHN, OTTO. *La Croisade contre le Graal.* Paris, 1934.

RAYNAUD, G. *Recueil de Motets Francais.* Le Chansonnier de Montpelier. Paris, 1881.

ROCHÉ, DÉODAT. *Les Cathares, Précurseurs des Temps Modernes.* Cahiers d'Etudes Cathares, 1963.

Catharisme et Science Spirituelle. Cahiers d'Études Cathares.

Contes et Légendes du Catharisme. Cahiers d'Études Cathares, 1966.

L'Église Romaine et les Cathares Albigeois. Cahiers d'Études Cathares, 1957.

RUNCIMAN, SIR STEVEN. *The Mediaeval Manichee.* Cambridge University Press, 1947.

SAINTSBURY, GEORGE. *French Lyrics.* Kegan, Paul, London, 1906.

SCHMIDT, C. *Histoire et Doctrine de la Secte Cathare ou Albigeois.* Paris-Genève, 1849.

SÖDERBERG. *La Religion des Cathares.*

STEPHEN, SIR JAMES. *Lectures on the History of France.* London, 1852.

THOUZELLIER, CHRISTIE. *Catharism et Valdeism en Languedoc.*

TODD, H. J. *History of the College of Bonshommes at Ashride,* 1823.

TURBERVILLE. *Mediaeval History and the Inquisition.*

VAISSETTE, DOM. *Histoire Génerale de Languedoc.*

INDEX

In the interests of precision I have excluded from this index certain references which constantly repeat themselves. These include such items as Catharism, re-incarnation, Roman Catholicism, Mrs. Smith, Roger, and Puerilia.